Unwrap Your Spiritual Gifts

KENNETH O. GANGEL

While this book is designed for the reader's personal enjoyment and profit, it is also intended for group study. A Leader's Guide with Victor Multiuse Transparency Masters is available from your local bookstore or from the publisher.

VICTOR BOOKS a division of SP Publications, Inc.

WHEATON, ILLINOIS 60187

Offices also in
Whitby, Ontario, Canada
Amersham-on-the-Hill, Bucks, England

Unless otherwise noted, Scripture quotations are from the *Holy Bible: New International Version* (NIV), © 1978 by the New York International Bible Society. Used by permission of Zondervan Bible Publishers. Other quotations are from the *New American Standard Bible* (NÁSB), © 1960, 1962, 1971, 1972, 1973 by The Lockman Foundation, La Habra, California; *The Living Bible* (LB), © 1971, Tyndale House Publishers, Wheaton, Illinois; *Holy Bible: Revised Standard Version* (RSV), © 1952 by the Division of Christian Education of the National Council of Churches of Christ in the United States; *The Amplified Bible* (AMP), © 1965 Zondervan Publishing House; and the *King James Version* (KJV).

Recommended Dewey Decimal Classification: 291.44
  Suggested Subject Heading: SPIRITUAL GIFTS

Library of Congress Catalog Card Number: 82-062220
ISBN: 0-88207-102-5

Contents

Foreword

The recovery of long-lost truth is as exciting and rewarding as the discovery of buried treasure. It even precipitates a gold rush of sorts, with many rushing to mount a caravan to the field of discovery, and others taking off helter-skelter, hoping with a minimum of equipment to cadge a nugget or two before the riches are gone.

As in all the gold rushes of history, only a fortunate few ever strike it rich. Usually they are the early comers or those who ignore the surface riches and seek steadily for the mother lode until they find it.

The whole subject of spiritual gifts is the lost treasure of 19th- and 20th-century Christianity. The church has been impoverished beyond belief by the prevailing ignorance of the existence of these spiritual riches. But now the long-buried truth is coming to light again. Widespread excitement has possessed the churches, and the tide of interest in the subject is running at full flow.

In this book, Dr. Kenneth Gangel has provided some splendid

examples of careful and profitable mining techniques. He pursues the mother lodes of Romans 12, 1 Corinthians 12, and other passages with productive skill and exposes the glowing truth to be found in each. He is especially helpful in giving practical ways to recognize personal spiritual gifts and in distinguishing between the real and the fool's gold which abounds today.

I commend this book to all who desire to enrich their lives by discovering all that God the Holy Spirit has buried in the hidden lodes of their lives in His sovereign distribution of the spiritual gifts.

Ray C. Stedman

1
Gifts and the Believer

Spiritual gifts have received increasing attention among evangelical Christians in recent years. Most of the books and articles dealing with the role of spiritual gifts in the contemporary church are either polemic or practical. Those with the polemic approach generally argue for or against what has been identified as the "charismatic position," favoring or opposing speaking in tongues and healing. The practical books are more concerned with the application of spiritual gifts in the church. Some are biblically oriented, while others on both sides of the charismatic issue are written from an experiential view. These authors argue points from what they have seen or felt regarding spiritual gifts.

It is not the purpose of this book to be controversial. While I hope these 12 chapters are practical, it is more important that they are biblical. We will explore the nature and use of the spiritual gifts named in the New Testament without concern for whether or not some have ceased with the completion of the New Testament canon. We will, however, assume that revelation ended when the New Testament was complete, and whatever gifts are available today are not the result of new inspired information from God.

What Are Spiritual Gifts?

It is unfortunate that neopentecostal influences have become known as the "charismatic movement." In applying the term in this way, we have allowed an important New Testament truth to be misused. The word *charisma* or *charismaton* is Greek for "spiritual gift." The word appears 17 times in the New Testament and can be grouped under three separate ideas: *God's gift of salvation* (Rom. 5:15–16; 6:23); *a general gift of grace or love* (Rom. 1:11; 2 Cor. 1:11; 7:7); *a specific endowment of spiritual ability for service* (Rom. 11:24; 12:6; 1 Cor. 1:7; 12:4, 9, 28, 30–31; 1 Tim. 4:14; 2 Tim. 1:6; 1 Peter 4:10).

The third usage is most prominent and the central passage is 1 Corinthians 12. Apart from 1 Peter 4:10, the word is used only by the Apostle Paul. We do well to note the connection between our word "charisma" and its root word *charis*. The latter means "grace" and suggests the proper basis for understanding how God gives gifts to His people.

The definition of *spiritual gifts* by the respected Greek lexicographer Thayer is as good as any: "extraordinary powers, distinguishing certain Christians and enabling them to serve the church of Christ, the reception of which is due to the power of divine grace operating in their souls by the Holy Spirit" (*A Greek Lexicon of the New Testament*, American Book Company, p. 667). My only hesitation in accepting this definition is the phrase "distinguishing certain Christians." If Thayer means "distinguishing one from another," I agree. If, however, he is implying that only certain Christians have spiritual gifts, such a view appears to be incompatible with New Testament teaching.

Paul clearly states that spiritual gifts are given *to every Christian* in the sovereignty of the Holy Spirit: "*to each one* is given" (1 Cor. 12:7, NASB). "He gives them *to each one,* just as he determines" (1 Cor. 12:11). "*We have different gifts,* according to the grace given us" (Rom. 12:6). (Italics in these Scripture references and in others throughout the book added.)

It would seem that every Christian has at least one spiritual gift, and some have more. Perhaps multi-gifted persons are placed by the Lord of the church into positions of leadership as pastors, evangelists, or teachers, and in other roles where such "clusters" of gifts are necessary.

The gift is probably not a ready-made ability to perform, but rather a capacity for service that must be developed. For example, a Christian with the gift of teaching should apply himself to training, reading, and practice to enable the Holy Spirit to produce competence in exercising his gift.

Charles Ryrie is right when he reminds us that we must not be too broad in applying the concept of gift. He says a spiritual gift "is not primarily a place of service ... a particular age-group ministry" (*The Holy Spirit*, Moody, p. 83). No one has the gift of India or the gift of youth work or of radio. What he may have is the gift of teaching and the call of God to use it with young people, or the gift of evangelism and the call of God to India.

What Is the Purpose of Spiritual Gifts?

On this question almost all evangelical scholars agree—spiritual gifts are given for the edification and spiritual growth of the church. "Edification is the practical test by which to decide on the admission of any manifestation of power into the church and estimate the comparative value of the gifts" (Thomas C. Edwards, *A Commentary on St. Paul's Epistles to the Corinthians,* Hodder & Stoughton, p. 312).

The relationship of chapters 12, 13, and 14 of 1 Corinthians is not accidental. The theme of this entire section is the body of Christ and its function in unity and love. *The possession and use of spiritual gifts is bound up with the functioning church.* One does not have the gift of evangelism to wander at will proclaiming the Gospel, but to relate that gift to the church—universal and local. Christ ministers to the body—the church—and it in turn ministers to the world.

The corporate use of gifts is basic. They are not given to "turn on" an individual, but to build up the total body. Though believers do not use their gifts only in the church building (not to be confused with the church body), the exercise of gifts and the ongoing ministry of the total body are inseparably related. Edification is the purpose; unity is the context; and love is the controlling principle or attitude for the proper exercise of spiritual gifts.

How Many Gifts?

This difficult question leads to two related questions: What are the specific gifts? Can they be categorized in any way? To both of these questions there are almost as many answers as commentators. In the traditional view, nine gifts are listed—all in 1 Corinthians 12:8-10. Most classical commentaries group these nine into three categories such as gifts of intellectual power, miraculous power, and tongues (Joseph Beet, *A Commentary on St. Paul's Epistles to the Corinthians,* Hodder and Stoughton, p. 215). Edwards opts for five: intellectual power, miraculous power, teaching power, critical power, and ecstatic power (*A Commentary,* p. 314).

Other scholars tend toward a greater number of gifts by taking into consideration all the passages. Theodore Epp lists 11 (*The Other Comforter,* Back to the Bible, pp. 81-91); Charles Ryrie, 14 (*The Holy Spirit,* pp. 83-91); John Walvoord, 15 (*The

Holy Spirit, Dunham, pp. 168–188); and Ray Stedman, "16 or 17 basic gifts, and these may be found in various combinations within a single individual; each cluster of gifts opening the door to a wide and varied ministry" (*Body Life,* Regal, p. 40).

As to categories, some refer to *permanent* and *temporary* gifts, *motivational, ministering,* and *manifestation* gifts, *inspired utterance, power* and *revelational* gifts, and *ordinary* and *extraordinary* gifts—to name a few.

In this book we will look at 20 gifts, but avoid arguments about their category or importance. Organization of the chapters is arbitrary. I have attempted simply to put together gifts which are related in terms of the kind of ministry they provide in the church. Obviously, to get a total of 20, I have recognized the *offices* of Ephesians 4:11 as gifts first given to men by the Spirit and then as gifted men given to the church by Christ. The following list, alphabetically arranged, *is* intended to be exhaustive. I believe that it includes all the gifts available to the church and needed by it today.

Administration	Knowledge
Apostleship	Leadership
Discernment	Mercy
Evangelism	Ministering
Exhortation	Miracles
Faith	Pastoring
Giving	Prophecy
Healing	Teaching
Hospitality	Tongues
Interpretation	Wisdom

Spiritual Gift or Natural Talent?

Theologically we can say that spiritual gifts work in the spiritual realm and natural talents in the natural realm. Since all Christians are human beings, they have natural talents as well as spiritual gifts. Since not all human beings are Christians, those who do not have the Holy Spirit cannot have spiritual gifts. Even a Christian might have a natural talent for public speaking but not necessarily have the gift of prophecy.

Natural abilities (talents) benefit the whole creation through common grace. Spiritual gifts, however, are largely limited to the church, though the presence and life of the church in the world are a benefit to mankind generally.

We must be careful to exercise spiritual gifts in the power of the Holy Spirit, for natural ability cannot generate spiritual ministry. Ray Stedman issues a valuable warning: "The lesson is clear. Don't try to use your natural talents to accomplish the work of God, for talents cannot operate in that sphere. But use them as channels or vehicles for spiritual gifts, and you will find that they dovetail beautifully. You might expect that they would do this since they both come from the same God" ("Equipped for Community," *His* magazine, Mar. '72, p. 3).

How Can You Know Your Spiritual Gifts?

Here are four brief but realistic guidelines for recognizing how the Holy Spirit has equipped you for service:

What do you enjoy doing? God *wants* you to be "happy in the service of the King." Christian ministry must not become a neurotic compulsion to duty. Findley Edge calls this the "eureka" principle, and Les Flynn writes about the "delight criterion."

How wrong to assume that because we enjoy some particular service that this ministry cannot be God's will for us. Or to deduce that because something is distasteful, this must be God's plan for us. Wouldn't God more likely assign us gifts the employment of which bring pleasure, not misery?

Like Jesus, in doing the Father's will we should find delight, not drudgery (*19 Gifts of the Spirit*, Victor, p. 201).

What service has God been blessing? Do you see fruit from your teaching? Are people trusting Christ as a result of your evangelism? It has been my exciting privilege for over two decades to watch college and seminary students discover their spiritual gifts through active involvement in ministry.

My teaching assistant served as an assistant pastor in a Hispanic church. His capability to communicate the Gospel cross-culturally (his family is Portuguese) brought forth fruit in amazing proportion. During the nine months of the school year, he witnessed to hundreds and several dozen people confessed Christ as Saviour.

On one occasion he went to a hospital to visit a parishoner. While there, he shared the Gospel with a visiting relative. Soon two or three other persons from nearby rooms gathered. Within 30 or 40 minutes, they had moved out into the hall, and this young college senior was preaching the Gospel to a small group at the end of that hospital wing. The group stayed until visiting hours were over. The interesting thing is that this young man is not particularly aggressive and may even lack self-confidence in some areas. The point is that God is blessing the gift of evangelism in his life.

How have others encouraged you? God gives us parents, pastors, teachers, and friends to help us in making key decisions like this. Local churches should probably be taking more initiative to assist members in identifying spiritual gifts.

One pastor on the East Coast preached a series of Sunday evening sermons on spiritual gifts and their application in the church. To culminate the series, he asked members of the congregation to stand and specify what gift or gifts each believed God had given him. No one was forced to do so, and some simply said they were not yet sure. After going around the room on that question, he asked folks to affirm or raise questions about the spiritual gifts identified by the persons next to them. No one was dogmatic, but some were able to confirm or deny the gifts mentioned.

What has the Holy Spirit told you? The inner witness of the Spirit is not limited to confirming our salvation. He *wants* us to know what our gifts are and how to use them.

Many ask, "When are spiritual gifts given?" Walvoord suggests that "spiritual gifts are bestowed at that time [spiritual baptism of the believer into the body] even if these gifts are not immediately observable" (*The Holy Spirit,* p. 166). Your gifts may be waiting to be activated. There may be reason to conclude that at times the Holy Spirit chooses to give a gift later in one's ministry, or for only a brief period of time (1 Tim. 4:14).

Can a Christian have any gift he wants? Not really. The sovereignty of the Spirit is decisive because He knows the needs of the church. But we do have an interesting verse which invites us to eagerly desire the greater gifts (1 Cor. 12:31). One thing is clear: *No gift is the sign of superior spirituality or a higher level of walk with God. The key is not so much to seek new gifts as to recognize, develop, and use the one(s) we have.*

There are two final questions to which I cannot provide answers. What is your spiritual gift? What are you doing about it? I hope that the following chapters will help you come to biblical and practical conclusions.

2
Administration and Leadership

Most everyone over age 20 will remember the television hit "Family Affair" even though it has been off the screen for years. In one episode, Uncle Bill had planned a night out, and a baby sitter was to arrive within minutes of Uncle Bill's departure to take care of Jody and Buffy until the next morning. The sitter failed to show, setting the stage for an evening of high jinks by the two small children.

After a hilarious dinner of just what you might expect, Jody took over to tuck in his little sister for the night. As he turned out the light and prepared to leave the room, Buffy asked, "Who will tuck *you* in?" Displaying his new-found chauvinism, Jody replied, "Nobody needs to. I'm in charge. Remember?" To which Buffy sighed and said, "I guess that's the trouble with people in charge. They have nobody to tuck them in."

People who have gifts of administration and leadership "have nobody to tuck them in." For a long time I questioned whether administration and leadership are separate gifts or different dimensions of the same gift, but now I see the gifts as two distinct but related types of equipping for ministry.

Students often ask the distinction between such words as *administration, management,* and *leadership.* No doubt writers use the words in different ways, but I would like to suggest that administration and management are synonymous. They are merely different terms used for varied approaches to the same process. For example, business and industry people tend to use the term *management* even when referring to churches and ministry. Educators, on the other hand, more often use *administration.* Schools and hospitals have *administrators,* but factories and law firms have *managers* or *managing partners.* The *city manager* of a community may very well have a master's degree in *public administration.*

Leadership is different. It is more identifiable by what a person *is* and administration or management by what he *does.* One thing is clear: people can be leaders without administering (the quarterback of a professional football team) and administrators without leading (scores of employees in the federal bureaucracy). It is important for us to see this distinction as we study these two gifts. Let's take them in alphabetical order.

The Gift of Administration

The Greek word for administration is *kubernēseis,* meaning helmsman or governor. All of its uses in Scripture refer to administration in some form of secular enterprise except where Paul impregnates the word with spiritual meaning and church context in 1 Corinthians 12:28. (Other uses appear in Proverbs 1:5; 24:6 of the *Septuagint* and Acts 27:11 and Revelation 18:17 in the New Testament.) It is a clear carry-over of the idea of organizing and superintending. The administrator is the person who is qualified to steer the ship. Gerhard Kittel puts it well when he refers to the Christian who is "a helmsman to his congregation, i.e., a true director of its order and therewith of its life" (*Theological Dictionary of the New Testament,* Eerdmans, Vol. 3, p. 1036).

How closely this gift is to be associated with pastoral ministry is difficult to establish. Most Baptist theologians link our present form of pastoral leadership to the New Testament offices of *episkopos* and *presbuteros,* frequently translated "bishop" in many English texts. Indeed, Archibald Robertson and Alfred Plummer suggest that the *kubernēseis* "may be equivalent to *episkopoi* and *presbuteroi*" (*The International Critical Commentary, 1 Corinthians,* Scribner's, p. 281).

I'm not so sure. In the first place, we are dealing here primarily with a gift, not an office which might arise out of a gift. Secondly, while it certainly would be advantageous for all pastors to have the gift of administration, there seems to be no solid biblical teaching indicating that this gift is *essential* for pastoral ministry. The point is that administration must be a part of orderly church life, and if the pastor is not gifted and trained in this aspect of spiritual ministry, who takes care of it?

The answer surely rests in the fact that most spiritual gifts are not limited to the officers of our churches. Every Christian has a spiritual gift, and an elder, a deacon, or a Sunday School superintendent might well be gifted by the Spirit for administrative ministry. It probably is not saying too much to suggest that we would do well to look for evidence of this gift when electing men to these and similar offices.

The idea that a layman could have the gift of administration finds scriptural basis as early as Exodus 18 where we read about Jethro, the first "management consultant." His proposal for reorganizing "the church in the wilderness" was a revelation to Pastor Moses. The revision placed emphasis on such time-honored administrative principles as span of control, definition of roles, decentralization, and delegation—to say nothing of the leadership development achieved by involving scores of other men in the administrative process.

Applying this principle will return a church to the genius of

New Testament congregations, namely, the dynamic of their lay leadership. One pastor friend of mine has not the slightest dose of the gift of administration and knows it. Consequently, he has committed all helmsman activities to lay leaders, freeing himself to concentrate on studying and proclaiming the Word. This is precisely the motivation which brought about naming the first deacons (Acts 6:1–6). According to Gene Getz,

> The selection of spiritually and psychologically qualified people for leadership positions in the church is one of the most obvious administrative principles in the New Testament. This is why most all the qualifications of elders and deacons in 1 Timothy 3 and Titus 1 relate to the man's reputation, ethics, morality, temperament, habits, and spiritual and psychological maturity (*Sharpening the Focus,* Moody Press, p. 151).

The Gift of Leadership

Let's look at leadership from the biblical perspective. The word, *prohistemi,* particularly as it appears in Romans 12:8 ("if it is leadership, let him govern diligently"), designates "one who is *set over* others, or who presides or rules," according to Commentator Albert Barnes (*Notes on the New Testament, 1 Corinthians,* Baker, p. 278). Surely if Paul had intended to mean administration again here, he could have used the word *kubernēseis.*

The word *prohistemi* appears eight times in Paul's writings, usually with an emphasis on personal leading of others and care for them. A key reference is 1 Timothy 3:4, where managing or ruling one's own house and family is identified as a prerequisite for pastoral ministry (cf. 1 Tim. 3:12; 5:8, 17). Some say that the context requires us to interpret that leadership is linked with the gifts of *giving* and *showing mercy,* which may be reference to the administration of charitable programs (Cranfield, Lagrange, Huby, Leenhardt).

Such a narrow application of the word, however, denies the broad usage in the Pauline epistles where it clearly is linked with coming forward, being set over, and ruling. One authoritative reference source suggests that in the early church, leadership emerged virtually separate from office.

The present writer believes there were as yet no institutionalized or precisely differentiated offices in the church known to Paul. He was influenced by the pattern of the charismatic community: "whoever is filled with zeal, whoever does not shirk hard work, proves himself thereby to be one who can lead the way for others" (H. Greeven, ZNW, 44, 34, cf. 32). This is confirmed by the list of gifts in Rom. 12:8, where the *prohistamenos* is characterized by *spoudē* (zeal). . . . All these words are participles which suggest an activity rather than an office (L. Coemen, *Dictionary of New Testament Theology,* Vol. 1, Zondervan, p. 197).

The context of Romans 12:8 is the movement from church liturgy to church leadership. With meekness, the church leader involves himself in concert with other believers to engage in ministry. There's no isolation here. The smog of selfishness and egoism must lift to make this mutual ministry a reality.

Why is it that the term *layman* too often carries negative connotations? If something is simplistic and elementary, we refer to it as being written in lay language. A secondary definition of the word *layman* in the *American Heritage Dictionary* is "one who does not have special or advanced training or skills." In the *Random House Dictionary* it is even worse: "One who is not a clergyman or one who is not a member of a specified profession; one who is not a member of the law or medicine." The general definition of layman is obvious—it is a person who is unable to do certain things. How diametrically opposed to biblical church order is such a distorted concept. The genius of lay leadership is inseparably related to the use of the gifts of leadership and administration. To be sure, not every appearance of the word *prohistemi* is a reference to the gift, just as no one would argue that every use of the Greek words for "teach" or "heal" is a reference to those spiritual gifts. But the linkup between leadership behavior at home and leadership responsibility in the church is unmistakable. My friend and former pastor writes:

In the sphere of the church, God's delegated human authority is given to elders for the purpose of overseeing and pastoring or shepherding. This is the picture given by Peter. "To the elders among you, I appeal as a fellow elder, a witness of Christ's sufferings and one who also will share in the glory to be revealed: be shepherds of God's flock that is under your care, serving as overseers" (1 Peter 5:1–2). This same emphasis is found in Hebrews: "Obey your leaders and submit to their authority. They keep watch over you as men who must give an account. Obey them so that their work will be a joy, not a burden, for that would be of no advantage to you" (Heb. 13:17). This is a proper use of spiritual authority which provides for the authoritative teaching of sound doctrine (A. Burge Troxel, "Accountability without Bondage: Shepherd Leadership in the Biblical Church," *Journal of Christian Education,* Spring, 1982, p. 197).

It seems to me that in a series on spiritual gifts one is dogmatic to his own peril. I prefer to think of these gifts as closely related, possibly united in a cluster for some church leaders, but not necessarily dependent one on the other. Edwards points out one thing we do well to keep in mind these days: "The government of the Corinthian church at this time was a pure democracy [in which] . . . the function of teaching was often separated from that of ruling" (*A Commentary on the First Epistle to the Corinthians,* Hodder and Stoughton, p. 335). And, I would add, the function of ruling was often separated from that of pastoring. The "strong man" monolithic churches of our day have frail basis in a proper understanding of New Testament gifts, even the necessary spiritual gift of administration.

3
Apostleship and Evangelism

To speak correctly of the task of missions in the late 20th century is to use the term *world evangelization.* The 1981 edition of *Unreached Peoples,* for example, includes a chapter entitled "The People-group Approach to World Evangelization" and the first paragraph speaks to the issue.

Because world evangelization is a task, it is essential to have a clear understanding of the goal of that particular task. The *nature* of world evangelization, in our opinion, is the communication of the Good News. The *purpose* of world evangelization is to give individuals and groups a valid opportunity to accept Jesus Christ. And the *goal* of world evangelization is the persuading of men and women to accept Jesus Christ as Lord and Saviour and serve Him in the fellowship of His church (C. Peter Wagner and Edward R. Dayton, David C. Cook, p. 19).

In New Testament times, evangelism meant the same thing, though the message was carried by sandaled missionaries walking across dusty roads rather than by religious broadcasts via satellite. One thing is clear from the Book of Acts: No separation can be made between the gift and/or office of *apostleship* and the task of *evangelism*. In speaking of the dynamic evangelism of the early church, J. Herbert Kane reminds us:

> Jesus chose 12 men, entrusted them with His truth, imbued them with His Spirit, invested them with His power, and sent them forth into the world. Everywhere and at all times they were to be as salt and light. They were to be different from other men, in character and conduct, in manners and morals, in motives and ideals; only so could they save the sinner, or reform society (*A Global View of Christian Missions,* Baker, p. 20).

The Gift of Apostleship

Is there a difference between the disciples and the apostles? Most evangelical scholars believe there is, and for textual reasons. The Great Commission commands a discipling of all nations, and gives the clear impression that all believers are called to a life of discipleship. The Twelve Apostles are frequently called disciples in the Gospels, but the term *apostle* is broadened in the early church.

The noun *apostolē* appears four times in the New Testament with no dramatic insight into the role of the gift (Acts 1:25; Rom. 1:5; 1 Cor. 9:2; Gal. 2:8). One reason for including apostleship in this book is the unique position of the idea in 1 Corinthians 12:28 and Ephesians 4:11. In both passages it is primarily viewed as an office, and perhaps that is Paul's only point of emphasis, but the intertwining relationship between gifts and offices in the New Testament leads me to explore the possibility of a gift of apostleship as well.

Originally the word *apostle* meant one who was commissioned as the commander of a fleet of ships. This interesting parallel with the gift of administration helps us to see the leadership stature inherent in the proper use of spiritual gifts. One chosen as an apostle would possess great authority, stand under direct orders from the chief of staff, and be required to travel extensively, often in foreign lands.

The New Testament use of the word does not depart widely from its basic root meaning. An apostle was one commissioned by the Lord, sent into the world under orders, with a specific message from his superior. "Messenger" conveys part of the concept, but fails to relate the authoritative nature of the apostolic gift.

During the days of the early church, the apostles equipped the saints by drawing them into working units, teaching them God's truth, and ordaining leaders for the local groups. Their lives were examples of holy living (1 Thes. 1), and their messages were viewed as authority by the young churches.

David L. Hocking and the staff of the First Brethren Church of Long Beach, California have prepared a helpful manual for teaching spiritual gifts in the church. In the section on apostles, they identify 10 qualities of those who exercised this gift in the first-century church. The apostle:

- Is one sent by a local church to other places (Acts 13:3–4).
- Seeks to lay a foundation in places where others have not worked (Rom. 15:20; 2 Cor. 10:16).
- Is under a great burden to preach the Gospel, and senses that he cannot be happy doing anything else.
- Is one who is willing to adapt to other cultures and lifestyles in order to win them to Christ (1 Cor. 9:19–22).
- Responds to doors of opportunity that are opened by the Lord (1 Cor. 16:8–9).
- Is recognized as a gifted man by other believers in the ministry of the local church (Acts 9:26–30; 11:25–26, 30; 12:25; 13:1–4; 1 Tim. 4:14).

- Seeks to start and develop churches with trained leadership that can carry on without him. (Acts 14:21–23; 2 Tim. 2:2).
- Is deeply concerned for the spiritual development of new believers (1 Thes. 2:1–12; 1 Cor. 4:14–17).
- Is one who is able to work under changing circumstances (1 Cor. 9:6–13; 2 Cor. 11:5–12).
- Is responsible for the doctrinal understanding and purity of the churches (Acts 20:18–32; 1 Tim. 2:4) (*Spiritual Gifts,* Sounds of Grace Ministries).

The Apostle Paul demonstrates the priority of this office in God's order of church life. Combining various apparent gifts with several offices, he exemplifies the blend of these two elements of spiritual dynamic. Frederick Godet wrote that "the apostolate continues the two sides of gift and office, both raised to their highest power" (*Commentary on St. Paul's First Epistle to the Corinthians,* T. and T. Clark, p. 225).

In Ephesians 4:11 we see this unique union. Men who have spiritual gifts *themselves* become spiritual gifts to the church. I assume that the five gift-offices mentioned in this verse can be considered gifts first, then offices.

Apostleship Now?

Can one possess the gift of apostleship in our day? John Lange is willing to stretch the term beyond the first century to apply to "those men, chosen and specially endowed by the Lord, appointed to found churches, as Boniface, the Apostle of the Germans; Egede, the Apostle of Greenland; Ziegenbalg and Schwartz, the Apostles of India" ("Ephesians," *A Commentary on the Holy Scriptures,* Zondervan, Vol. 21, p. 149).

Boniface lived in the eighth century, and Ziegenbalg was taking a furlough as late as 1715. So why not think of Carey and Judson as apostles, and with a bit of flexibility, church-planting missionaries on almost every continent today?

Of greater concern to us than Lange's views, however, is the use of the concept of apostleship in the New Testament. The noun *apostolos* occurs in Matthew 10:2, Mark 6:30, and five times in Luke (6:13; 9:10; 17:5; 22:14; 24:10). In the Gospels the term is simply a synonym for the disciples. In all likelihood, what we are seeing is the use of a term which was familiar at the time of writing (much later than the life and ministry of our Lord) but was not necessarily in use at the time the incidents actually happened. The many uses in Acts refer to the Twelve, to Matthias, and of course to Paul. Barnabas is also called an apostle (14:14), though by the time John wrote the Revelation, the number is down to 12 (21:14). It seems clear, however, that the office was quite fixed, for the New Testament never indicates an intention to confer "the apostolate" as an institutionalized church office, passed on from generation to generation. Whether there were 11, 12, 14, or more, the number was clearly limited. Consequently, most evangelicals feel very uncomfortable using the term *apostle* to describe any office or leader in the church today.

Is it possible, however, for us to conceive of a separation of gift and office after the first century? Rather than assigning this gift to the history of the early church, can we not recognize the broad sense of the verb form *apostellō* ("to send on a mission")? Could it not be that in the time between the 1st and 20th centuries the Holy Spirit has given this gift to God's people in what we have come to call *missionary service?*

The verb *apostellō* is used 131 times in the New Testament with most of the references spread somewhat evenly among the Gospels and Acts. Though we may not have apostles in the church-office sense, we are witnessing in the last two decades of the 20th century the greatest going out of "servants-with-a-message" the world has ever known.

Many have chosen the option of locking several of the spiritual gifts into the first century, lest some explanation be required for their presence in the church today. I would prefer to allow the Holy Spirit the broadest latitude to produce in Christ's body any gift in any age as He sees fit. It seems quite safe to say that the *office* of the apostles was restricted to the establishing of the New Testament church. But if Lange is right in stretching the term through missionary history, we may be justified in seeing evidence of "apostleship" not only as a gift, but as a gift which has operated in the church throughout all the years of its history.

The Gift of Evangelism

As unusual as it may seem, the word "evangelist" (*euangelistes*) appears only three times in the New Testament (Acts 21:8; Eph. 4:11; 2 Tim. 4:5). The word should not be construed to mean "soul-winner," because it conveys only the more specific delineation of communicating the Gospel, that is, "one who shares the Good News." William Barclay refers to evangelists as "the rank and file missionaries of the church" (As quoted by Francis Foulkes, *The Epistle of Paul to the Ephesians,* Eerdmans, p. 119).

Of the three texts mentioned, Ephesians 4:11 is the only one which includes evangelism on the list of the spiritual gifts. It is possible, as I suggested earlier, that these refer to offices and not to gifts. I believe, however, that the relationship of these ministries to previously mentioned charisms is sufficient evidence that the persons referred to in verse 11 have been first gifted in accordance with the pattern of 1 Corinthians 12 and then, given as gifts to the church.

The itinerant nature of first-century evangelists is exemplified by Philip (Acts 8). The evangelist proclaimed the redemptive message of the Gospel in an area and then moved on to proclaim it in another. Meanwhile, the local pastors and teachers set about the task of edifying the congregation.

It appears that sometimes the same individual was both evangelist and teacher. Paul, for example, planted churches on the first missionary journey (evangelism) which he nurtured and built up in the faith on the second trip (teaching). Timothy was probably a pastor-teacher at Ephesus, yet Paul wrote and reminded him to "do the work of an evangelist" (2 Tim. 4:5).

Two peripheral yet important ideas connected with spiritual gifts bear mentioning here. First, we should ask whether it is possible to have a spiritual gift "for a time," that is, on a temporary basis. Apparently evangelism was not Timothy's primary gift, but he was to engage in it as a part of his other duties.

Dr. George Peters of Dallas Theological Seminary told a story about his own ministry. It is related here from memory, so all details may not be completely accurate. Apparently a mission representative from a South American country called to ask Dr. Peters if he could spend some time during the summer ministering on that field. Dr. Peters responded affirmatively until he understood that the task would be to conduct evangelistic campaigns. Then the conversation went something like this:

"I'm sorry, but I'm afraid I shouldn't come. You see, I have the gift of teaching, not the gift of evangelism."

"But, Dr. Peters, if we pray that God will give you the gift of evangelism for the ministry here, and if you believe He has answered our prayer, will you accept our invitation?"

"Yes, if you put it that way. Let's see how the Holy Spirit responds."

Dr. Peters testifies that he received the gift of evangelism for that month of ministry only. In the fall he returned to teaching.

No one likes to build a theology of experience less than I, but if we recognize the Holy Spirit's sovereign control over spiritual gifts, we must allow for temporary gifting for specific, short-term service.

Another point of caution here is that one does not need to have the full gift of a ministry in order to follow God's command to serve. Not every Sunday School teacher has the *gift* of teaching, but the Spirit still can enable such persons to carry out an effective ministry. Actually, every Christian parent is required to be a teacher, but not every Christian parent has the gift of teaching.

Walvoord points out the same about evangelism: "While all are called to bring the Gospel to the lost by whatever means may be at their disposal . . . it is the sovereign purpose of God that certain men should have a special gift in evangelism" (*The Holy Spirit,* Dunham Publishing, p. 170). To put it very simply, we do not have to be Billy Grahams in order to share our faith with others.

John MacPherson suggests that the term *evangelist* (like *apostle* and *prophet*) designated a high office in the first-century church, and "though the offices were not continued, many of the most characteristic of the gifts which qualified for these offices are found to be in the possession of individual holders of the permanent ministerial office" (*Commentary on St. Paul's Epistle to the Ephesians,* T. and T. Clark, p. 309). This may be a significant clue to understanding how our spiritual gifts operate today. Before the completed canon, it was essential for the church to have authoritative revelation from God, so that possessing many of the gifts was tantamount to holding office. Now God *has* spoken through His written Word, and we can understand what He has said about gifts and explain it to others.

With the possible exception of Timothy's unique ministry, which was as an overseer in several congregations, almost all references to evangelism and evangelists focus on people outside the organized congregations. The early churches emphasized worship, nurture of Christians, and fellowship—there's no need to evangelize believers. Yet today, too often we think of the church building as the place for people to "get saved."

The ministry of Philip (Acts 8) is a marvelous example of a layman in action as a representative of the gathered church. Philip was sensitive to the Spirit's leading and moved from place to place accordingly. He was adaptable—any town, anytime—ready to preach, pray, or die in the name of Jesus. He was ready with the appropriate word of the Gospel, able to expound God's Word at a moment's notice. It is easy to identify Philip with the gift of evangelism.

Perhaps in the twilight years of the 20th century, we are seeing a revival of one-to-one witnessing, a resurgence of the faith-sharing which characterized the early churches. Perhaps we are seeing a fresh awareness of the significance of this spiritual gift as well, whether used among neighbors or in a foreign culture and in a new language.

4
Exhortation and Prophecy

Today the city is called Antakiyeh and it is only a shade of its former self. It was constructed in 301 B.C. and became the capital of Syria. Indeed, 16 cities bearing the same name were constructed in honor of the Seleucid emperor, Antiochus, but only Antioch of Syria, that great commercial center of the ancient world, rose to prominence. In 65 B.C., with a population of 500,000, it was the third largest city in the empire.

In the Scriptures we see Antioch as the mother of all churches, the first truly mixed congregation of Jews and Greeks whose concern for world evangelization spawned not one but three missionary journeys. Its first leader was Barnabas, the "son of encouragement," nicknamed by the church at Jerusalem because of his apparent consistency in exercising the gift of exhortation.

I have steadfastly resisted an attempt to group the gifts lest some artificial categorizing be superimposed on the biblical text. It is obvious, however, that there are several gifts which have to do with speaking to others, either publicly or privately.

These are teaching, offering a word of wisdom, sharing a word of knowledge, prophecy, and exhortation. The two gifts before us in this chapter are alike in that they both entail speaking to others; they are different in that one can be implemented privately and the other, publicly.

The Gift of Exhortation

When Jesus tried to teach the disciples about His coming death, resurrection, and ascension, they found it hard to face even the thought of His absence. "Lord, to whom shall we go?" reflected their concern and the childlike quality of their faith throughout their three-and-one-half years with the incarnate Lord.

Seeking to alleviate their fear of the unknown, as well as to teach them some basic pneumatology, the Master explained that the Father would be sending "another Counselor" (John 14:16). We have come to know the Greek term used in this passage to describe the Holy Spirit as the word *paraclete* (one who is called alongside to comfort and counsel). Two similar forms of this word appear in Romans 12:8 to introduce the charism (gift) of exhortation and are rendered, "If it is encouraging, let him encourage" (NIV).

The verb form (*parakaleō*) appears 108 times in the New Testament, while the noun *paraklēsis* (encouragement) appears 29 times, and the word *paraklētos* 5 times. A similar term, generally rendered "comfort," is the Greek word *paramuthia*, and it appears 6 times. David L. Hocking suggests the similarity:

The distinction between *parakaleō* and *paramutheomai* seems to be very slight. Both words use the preposition *para* and carry the idea of "alongside of" or the person-to-person ministry. *Parakaleō* is best reflected by the English word "exhortation" if you understand that its basic motivation is "to help." *Paramutheomai* seems best translated as "comfort," in the sense of encouragement and reassurance (*Spiritual Gifts,* Sounds of Grace Ministries).

Throughout Scripture the concept of exhortation has a double meaning: to comfort or encourage, and to admonish. Rather than stressing one and minimizing the other, we can profit by remembering the family references seen in Scripture. A good father is depicted as regularly engaged in both aspects of exhortation, sometimes in connection with the same incident. The Apostle Paul used the father image for one in a leadership role of the church. "For you know that we dealt with each of you as a father deals with his own children, encouraging, comforting, and urging you to live lives worthy of God, who calls you into His kingdom and glory" (1 Thes. 2:11–12).

In the arena of congregational life, there is a constant need for pastors to exercise the gift of *paraklēsis* (exhortation). Paul frequently called the believers together for exhortation, which was usually a combination of challenge and comfort (Acts 11:23; 14:22; 15:32). The gift is closely (but not inseparably) connected with the gift of prophecy (1 Cor. 14:31; 1 Tim. 4:13–14)—another indication that it is often exercised within the pastoral office.

In studying the original text of Romans 12, I am impressed by the fact that this same word *parakaleō* appears in verse 1, translated in the *King James Version* by the English word "beseech" and in the *Revised Standard Version,* "appeal." The *New International Version* uses the word "urge," and indeed, the strong sense of urgency implies that the Christian's use of the gift of exhortation is not only passive and nondirective encouragement, but also explicit advice.

This leads me to mention the current controversy over the role and procedures of the Christian counselor. In secular psychology, the revolt against the purely nondirective pattern has been led by such reality therapists as William Glasser and O.

Hobart Mowrer. Evangelicals have been introduced to this individual responsibility theme through Jay Adams' *Competent to Counsel* (Baker). (The same basic thrust is seen in the writings of Walter Trobisch.) Adams talks about "nouthetic counseling" and "confrontation," emphasizing the role of God's absolute truth in dealing with the counselee's problems.

One does not need to opt for exclusively directive or nondirective counseling to recognize that the gift of *paraklēsis* relates to both. Counseling is a process, not a gift, so it would be improper to equate the two and identify *paraklēsis* as "the gift of counseling." The gift has a broader application in preaching, teaching, and informal conversations among believers. It may very well be, however, that as certain people gifted in *euangelistes* become "evangelists," so persons gifted in *paraklēsis* become "counselors."

Public and Private Ministry

Exhortation is therefore both a public and a private ministry. It is limited neither to pulpit nor pew, to leader nor layman. I know a young Christian mother who has been through extreme physical suffering. Now the Holy Spirit causes her to cross paths with others just as they learn of some tragedy in their own lives. She may very well have the gift of exhortation in being able to encourage persons going through suffering, and perhaps in giving them counsel as well.

Perhaps another common use of the gift is through song. There is no "gift of music" in the strict sense of charisma. Music is a general grace to all mankind. But "singing and making melody" (Eph. 5:19, NASB), when the theology is sound and the musician Spirit-filled, is surely a superb way of exhorting the church in public ministry. Choir members, neglect not the gift that may be in you!

It is interesting how the gift of exhortation in the New Testament is so frequently linked with the ministry of the local church. Barnabas practiced it at Jerusalem and at Antioch. Judas and Silas exhorted the believers at Antioch after the Council of Jerusalem (Acts 15:31–32). Paul exhorted the Ephesian elders in one of the longest displays of the gift of exhortation seen in Scripture (Acts 20:17–35). Perhaps Larry Crabb has the gift of exhortation well in mind when he proposes that "caring, mature Christian people (who can love because they know Christ's love, and who are mature because they desire above all else to know Him) can become capable counselors within their local church bodies." He continues:

With an enthusiasm restrained by some awareness of the problems involved, I envision the development of meaningful counseling within the local church carried on by church members. When it is operating biblically, the body of Christ provides individuals with all the necessary resources to appropriate their significance and security in Christ. But we must not think that opportunities for ministry (which meet security needs) automatically will be seized upon eagerly by every believer and clearly understood as relevant to their basic needs. . . . The local church must assume responsibility for the individual personal care of each member. Obviously no ministerial staff can deal adequately with the staggering needs for individual attention and concern within the body. Nor should it even try to. The job belongs to the members of the local body (*Effective Biblical Counseling,* Zondervan, pp. 163–64).

Crabb surely is not implying that every church member has the gift of exhortation. But some do, and they are not necessarily all members of the pastoral staff.

Because of the close connection between "teaching" and "exhortation" in Romans 12, and their common ultimate purpose (edification), some have thought to tie them together more closely than the text may imply. Teaching focuses on communicating content, whereas exhortation, to borrow C. E. Cranfield's phrase, "is to help Christians to live out their obedience to the Gospel" (*A Commentary on the Holy Scriptures,* Oliver and Boyd, p. 33). Martin Luther once noted, "Teaching and exhortation differ from each other in this, that teaching is directed to the ignorant but exhortation to those who have knowledge" (*Lectures on Romans,* The Library of Christian Classics, Vol. 15, 5:336). And Albert Barnes helpfully adds, "This word (*paraklēsis*) properly denotes one who urges to the practical duties of religion, in distinction from one who teaches its doctrines. One who presents the warnings and promises of God to excite men to the discharge of their duty" (*Notes on the New Testament,* Baker, p. 273).

These are days of people emphasis in our churches. We are turning away from a focus on programs to a more biblical focus on people. It is a good time to reconsider, restore, and refresh the gift of exhortation among our congregations, not only in sermon and private office, but also in the sharing of individual believers from house to house, seeking to mutually edify in love.

The Gift of Prophecy

The church at Corinth was planted during the second missionary journey immediately after Paul left Athens. Corinth was one of the most wicked cities of its day—so much so that the term "Corinthian" came to be synonymous with immorality and sexual perversion. Awareness of the nature of the city helps us to understand the church to which Paul wrote two epistles. This understanding is most strategic in grasping Paul's emphasis on the use of the gift of prophecy in that congregation. After listing the spiritual gifts in great detail, and relating them to the unity of the body of Christ (1 Cor. 12), Paul pauses to emphasize how all spiritual gifts must be administered in an attitude and atmosphere of love (1 Cor. 13). Then in an immediate transition, come these words: "Let love be your greatest aim; nevertheless, ask also for the special abilities the Holy Spirit gives, and especially the gift of prophecy, being able to preach the messages of God" (1 Cor. 14:1, LB).

The apostle suggests that the genuinely mature Christian should understand the significance of prophecy and its relationship to tongues, and that such understanding is the mark of spiritual adulthood (14:20). Never one to miss an opportunity for practical application, Paul indicates that the wise Christian will be naive concerning evil, but will be most mature concerning the issues of the Christian life, specifically in the use of spiritual gifts. He warns that one does not examine evil even in the worthy name of research. He learns what he needs to know about evil from God's Word rather than by dabbling in various kinds of sin, such as the occult, and/or other areas in Satan's domain.

The word *prophēteia* comes from the verb *prophēmi,* which means "to speak forth." When defining any word of Scripture, one must take into consideration two extremely important factors: *etymology* (the basic derivation of the word) and *use.* Sometimes they differ greatly, and most scholars agree that use at the time of the word's appearance takes precedence in determining its meaning. In this case, however, there is no great difference between the derivation of the word and its use. The idea of speaking forth, particularly speaking forth the Word of God, is common wherever the word appears. The problem comes when we link New Testament with Old Testament usage. The Old Testament prophet was primarily a *foreteller* whose task and ministry was to proclaim future events. That aspect of the word is not absent from New Testament usage but, as the great Greek scholar Gerhard Kittel suggests, the idea of prediction in the word is really a "special sense," and one which "occurs chiefly in Revelation" (*Theological Dictionary of the New Testament,* 6:830).

The word appears in its various forms 200 times in the New Testament. It refers to almost every aspect of both revelatory and nonrevelatory proclamation. The proclamation of God's truth is not necessarily a foretelling of the future. Colin Brown reminds us that "when one examines the combination of *pro-* with verbs of speech in earlier writings, it is evident that in no case does the object of the verb point to the future. . . . The meaning of these verbs is clearly to proclaim openly, to state publicly, to proclaim aloud. This suggests that *prophēteuō* should be translated in the same way. This is corroborated by the use, found as early as the fifth century, of *prophēteis* in the sense of declarer, speaker" (*Dictionary of New Testament Theology,* Vol. 3, pp. 74–75).

Early in the New Testament, prophecy was largely personal inspiration as God's revelation came directly to men like Peter and Paul. As the gift began to be used with regularity in the established congregations, it quickly became more of an analysis of written revelation. A. T. Robertson refers to it as "speaking forth God's message under the guidance of the Holy Spirit" (*Word Pictures in the New Testament,* Vol. 4, Harper, 4:403). If I were to attempt a short and understandable definition, it would be something like this: *Prophecy* is congregational preaching which explains and applies God's revelation.

The central passage dealing with the use of the gift of prophecy rises above all other texts on the subject. It is Paul's injunction to the Corinthian believers (1 Cor. 14) where at least four guidelines are found.

Emphasis on Prophecy

Indeed, we could say that prophecy is of primary importance with respect to the public ministry of the church. Paul is very clear, "Desire ... that you may prophesy" (v. 1, NASB); "I want you all to speak in tongues, but even more to prophesy" (v. 5); "So, my brethren, earnestly desire to prophesy" (v. 39). In 12:28 he lists the role of the prophet immediately after that of the apostle in the hierarchy of importance for the ministry of the church.

There is a practical reason for all this. Prophecy produces the kinds of results which are absolutely necessary if we are to have spiritually equipped and mature Christians in our churches. Here is the clue: "He who prophesies speaks to men for their upbuilding and encouragement and consolation" (1 Cor. 14:3, RSV).

It took me a long time to realize how many times the idea of Christian edification is mentioned in this chapter. It is virtually a dominating theme appearing with emphasis in verses 3, 4, 5, 12, 17, and 26. One might very well say that 1 Corinthians 14 is not primarily about tongues or prophecy, but rather about an upbuilding ministry in the church!

It is important to take care in the public exercise of this gift (or any other) that its purpose be to benefit people. Star performer or VIP attitudes should not characterize the one who prophesies. Rather, he should speak the message of God under the control of the Holy Spirit for the upbuilding of the church. The three elements of prophecy—upbuilding, encouragement, and consolation—are much needed in the contemporary church. We have many discouraged Christians who need encouragement. Millions—Christians among them—are flocking to counselors, psychologists, and psychiatrists in search of peace and comfort in troubled times. Entire congregations are starving spiritually because their weekly diet contains insufficient calories to sustain any decent measure of spiritual health. Exercise of the gift of prophecy was not only important to the church of Corinth in the first century; it is a prime need in the evangelical church today.

Prophecy Is Primarily for Believers

Tongues are used as a sign to those who do not believe the Gospel. Prophecy, on the other hand, is aimed primarily at those who have already trusted Christ and are members of God's family through regeneration. This is also a major difference between prophetic preaching and evangelistic preaching. Evangelistic preaching centers on salvation by faith in Christ through the grace of God, whereas prophetic preaching deals with the total revelation of God. Evangelistic preaching is directed to the unsaved and is, in that sense, very definitely "missionary" in scope. Prophetic preaching, on the other hand, is aimed at saved people and exercised in the gatherings of the community of the redeemed which we call local churches.

I recall the Saturday in 1968 which ended the week in which Sen. Robert Kennedy was assassinated. The funeral had engrossed the media throughout the day, and at 11:30 P.M., a weary Chet Huntley and David Brinkley were bringing to a close their long coverage. Their frustrations were evident in their personal comments: "What kind of people are we? How can this type of thing happen? What is the world coming to?" Without any answers they signed off—"Good night, Chet. Good night, David. Good night for NBC news."

As I turned off the TV I remarked to my wife, "I can't wait for church tomorrow when we can hear a prophet of God proclaim answers to questions secular newsmen can't handle."

Abortion, infanticide, international terrorism, rape, epidemic venereal disease, deviant marital forms—these and a host of other social maladies provide opportunities and reasons to proclaim God's truth with application to present-day problems and needs.

Prophecy Can Be Evangelistic

Since prophetic preaching deals with the total revelation of God, it also deals with the essential elements of the Gospel, and for that reason can be at times evangelistic. Evangelism is not its primary purpose, but is a fringe benefit. The Apostle Paul says:

> But if an unbeliever or someone who does not understand comes in while everybody is prophesying, he will be convinced by all that he is a sinner and will be judged by all, and the secrets of his heart will be laid bare. So he will fall down and worship God, exclaiming, "God is really among you" (1 Cor. 14:24–25).

Prophetic preaching is evangelistic because it produces conviction, judgment, and spiritual awareness. It is quite common in our day to see people who are really born again become disenchanted with their attendance at liberal churches where there is no solid prophetic preaching. Because they have not been fed spiritual food, they are still babes in the things of God's revelation, even though they may have been Christians for a number of years. Invariably, what attracts them to a vital evangelical congregation is not the building, the program, or even the friendliness of the people, but rather their hunger for expository preaching.

Jack W. MacGorman identifies four specific steps described in this passage and details how the gift of prophetic preaching affects the unbeliever attending such a public service.

> He is convicted by all. As God's truth is proclaimed and as witness is borne to it by gifted and faithful servants, the unbeliever is convicted of his sinful condition before God. (Cf. John 16:8 where the same verb occurs.) He is called to account by all who speak.
>
> The secrets or hidden things of his heart are exposed. No man ever sees himself as he appears to God until the Spirit of God lays bare his heart.
>
> Convicted of sin and with his heart bared, he falls on his face before God to worship Him.

He exclaims joyously: "God is certainly among you!" (1 Cor. 14:25, NASB). From unbelief to conviction, confession, and worship—all in one service (*The Gifts of the Spirit,* Broadman, p. 104).

Multiple Prophets

The Plymouth Brethren have been telling us for a long time that most of us in mainline denominations have missed the point of the New Testament's emphasis on multiple ministry. Though their lack of form may have become a form in itself, they perhaps offer more of a handle on New Testament patterns than we have been willing to admit. Total involvement of God's people in ministry is certainly the desired result of developing and using spiritual gifts. In terms of prophecy, we tend to identify only one congregational preacher, and the rest of us become resigned to audience behavior. However, Paul says, "Let *two* or *three* prophets speak" (v. 29, NASB), and "but if *all* prophesy" (v. 24, NASB). We cannot pass over this multiple emphasis.

It seems that today more congregations are experimenting with alternatives to the one-man pulpit. The sharing of the preaching ministry with others who have the gift of prophecy is a valid New Testament option, and allowing response to preaching seems to be well in line with the end of verse 29: "Others should weigh carefully what is said."

In recognizing that many may exercise the gift of prophecy, we see that the gift is under the rational control of each prophet. To be specific, utterances do not come pouring ecstatically out of a man as he sits in the 17th pew at the Sunday evening service. "Remember that a person who has a message from God has the power to stop himself or wait his turn" (14:32, LB). Multiple ministry in using the gift of prophecy does not consist of confusion, noise, or pandemonium. It is logical, quiet, and orderly. Otherwise it does not emanate from God (v. 33).

Women Prophets?

What about the question of women prophets? According to the New Testament, there is no doubt that women had the gift of prophecy. Philip's daughters, for example, exercised the gift (Acts 21:8–9). Though women may have the gift of prophecy, there seems to be little New Testament precedent for the exercise of that gift *in the congregation.* "The women should keep silence in the churches" (1 Cor. 14:34) may refer to the use of the two gifts of prophecy and tongues, though some reputable commentators suggest an application to the disruptive chatter of women in the synagogues.

I take the position that ordination of women is not biblical. On the other hand, women may indeed have the gift of prophecy, and they may exercise it in many avenues such as ministry in Bible classes and in the Sunday School, as well as at home. Siegfried Grossmann contrasts two mothers.

Let us assume that two mothers have received the gift of prophecy through prayer and laying on of hands. One of them has a natural gift for teaching and her training is already above average. The other mother has great difficulties training her children and is at the end of her strength. Through prophetic words and decisions, both will sense that difficult situations are easier to handle. Both will still have difficulties with their children, but their progress will please them. The change in the pedagogically talented mother is less impressive than in the other, but the Holy Spirit's endowment is readily recognized in the greater strength of both (*There Are Other Gifts Than Tongues,* Tyndale, pp. 21–22).

Perhaps exercising the gift of prophecy in the corporate congregational life of the church would tend to violate a woman's prior principle of submissiveness and obedience. This is the contrast Paul makes (vv. 34–35).

Results of properly using the gift of prophecy in the modern congregation will not be greatly different from those in the first century. The local church will reflect order, peace, encouragement, consolation, conviction, spiritual awareness, and learning. Above all, exercising the gift of prophecy results in spiritual upbuilding—the primary task of the church.

5
Tongues and Interpretation

There is no issue so controversial and divisive in evangelical Christianity today as that of speaking in tongues. Dr. Kenneth Kantzer suggests that "the last third of 20th-century church history may be remembered as 'The Revival of Charismatic Gifts.'" Total world membership in pentecostal bodies is estimated at more than 10 million, and Kantzer suggests that when charismatics in mainline Protestant denominations are added to that total, it is safe to say that figures for those who claim to have spoken in tongues or who regularly participate in meetings where the gift is practiced probably run much higher ("The Tongues Movement of Today: Bane or Blessing," *Trinity Today,* October, 1971, p. 6).

Articles and books on the gift of tongues abound; therefore, in the following paragraphs I will only attempt to help readers sort out the crucial questions which must be asked for an intelligent understanding of the issue, and to review the significant passages of Scripture on the subject.

Few subjects can change fellowship to fury among evangelicals more rapidly than a discussion of tongues. Some are rigidly opposed. Popular pastor and radio preacher, John MacArthur, Jr. says, "After seven years of studying the question and reading all sides of the issue, and discussing it with charismatics as well as noncharismatics, I am convinced beyond any reasonable doubt that tongues ceased in the Apostolic Age and that when they stopped, they stopped for good" (*The Charismatics,* Zondervan, p. 166). On the other hand, popular pastor and author, Leslie B. Flynn warns that "to class all tongues-speaking today as spurious is daring, dangerous, and a denial of the right of the sovereign Spirit to endow His servants with whatever gift He pleases" (*19 Gifts of the Spirit,* Victor, p. 181).

If it is possible to put aside any *a priori* conclusions as we approach such an emotion-filled subject, let's consider three basic questions: What is the gift of tongues? What is the purpose of the gift? What are the biblical guidelines for its use?

What Is the Gift of Tongues?

Actually this question leads to several others. It becomes immediately essential to identify the nature of the gift of tongues in each of the instances in which it appears in Scripture, and then to compare the biblical gift and the one practiced today. There are two options in each case: The gift of tongues enabled one to speak either in unlearned languages or in ecstatic utterances. Though there are strong opinions on each side, the weight of evidence leans toward an understanding of tongues as unlearned languages, both in the three crucial Acts passages (2:1–42; 10:1–48; 19:1–7) and in the experience of the Corinthian church (1 Cor. 12—14).

In question is the Greek word *glōssa*. This is clearly the word for "language," and only a unique contextual interpretation would lead one to conclude that the reference is to ecstatic utterance. Yet Dr. Charles Smith writes:

All the evidence suggests that biblical tongues were in all cases ecstatic utterances and essentially unintelligible. Any such utterances (today as well) may occasionally have included foreign words or phrases, but these were only bits and pieces in the mass of unrecognizable sounds (*Tongues in Biblical Perspective,* BMH Books, p. 40).

A more common view is suggested by Walvoord, who says that "any view which denies that speaking in tongues used actual languages is difficult to harmonize with the scriptural concept of a spiritual gift" (*The Holy Spirit,* Dunham, p. 182).

Some commentators attempt to make a distinction between the passages in the Book of Acts and the one in 1 Corinthians, indicating that in Acts tongues speakers used languages, but at Corinth the gift had degenerated into meaningless ecstatic utterance. Sometimes 1 Corinthians 14:2 ("he utters mysteries with his Spirit") is used to support this view. In the situation at Corinth, however, it seems that some were using the gift without interpretation. When there is no interpreter, a tongue becomes an unknown mystery which no one understands. Kittel puts it this way:

The uncontrolled use of tongues might thus make it appear that the community is an assembly of madmen (14:23, 27). Yet tongues are a legitimate sign of overwhelming power (14:22). There are various kinds (12:10, 28; cf. 14:10); some are tongues of men and others of angels (13:1). To make *glossolalia* serviceable in the community, however, either the speaker or another brother must be able to give an interpretation (14:5, 13, 27f; 12:10, 30). In Corinth, therefore, *glossolalia* is an unintelligible ecstatic utterance (*Theological Dictionary of the New Testament,* Eerdmans, 1:722).

It seems that attempts to make *glōssa* mean something different in 1 Corinthians than it does in the Book of Acts are suspect and rest on fragile evidence.

We still have the question of whether *contemporary* tongues are ecstatic utterances or languages. Certainly if one concludes that the biblical gift is exclusively a reference to speaking in unlearned languages, persons who claim to speak in tongues as ecstatic utterance would fail to qualify as possessing the gift. At this point, it is up to the charismatic movement to demonstrate in some way that contemporary tongues are languages.

Some have called for scientific investigation, such as the offer by those who have the gift to allow linguists to examine its properties. I am not convinced scientific investigation can be used. In some cases, such as salvation by faith, corroboration is virtually impossible.

Stanley Gundry claims that if we subtract all the tongues speakers who admit to using ecstatic utterance rather than unlearned languages, "most claims to *glossolalia* could be rejected on this basis alone" ("Facing the Issues of Tongues," *Moody Monthly,* Oct. 1973, p. 100). I'm not sure this statement can be supported, but certainly the issue of recognizing what speaking in tongues is or is not is crucial.

Those interested in researching further the issue of contemporary *glossolalia* will want to check William J. Samarin's book, *Tongues of Men and Angels* (Macmillan). Samarin is a Christian linguist whose research in the area of modern tongues speakers has convinced him that contemporary tongues are basically not languages. Samarin also concludes that the tongues referred to in 1 Corinthians were not real languages either. He believes the early Christians practiced ecstatic utterance much in the way that it is used in the present day. So after a quick wheel around the circle, we are back where we started.

What Was the Purpose of Tongues?

We could reasonably assume that God's purpose in giving the gift initially would be the same for contemporary tongues if they are truly a demonstration of the spiritual gift. Perhaps in attempting to answer this question, it is important at the outset to recognize what the gift of tongues is *not.* Nothing in Scripture indicates that the gift of tongues signals some special evidence such as the baptism of the Holy Spirit. To think that any one gift should be normative for all Christians, or that it should represent some high level of spiritual maturity is diametrically opposed to the very nature of the sovereign issuing of spiritual gifts. The fact that the carnal and divisive congregation at Corinth apparently made ample use of the gift of tongues indicates that its presence does not denote special spirituality, and conversely, its absence does not denote any lack of spirituality or failure to have a special experience which God wants every Christian to have.

Yielding to the Spirit in letting Him fill us brings different reactions in different people. Some find it exhilarating, joyous, as if a load has been lifted. Others may find that nothing seems to happen emotionally, but they feel a peace and a satisfaction that can come no other way. Whatever our reactions might be, the Scriptures make it plain that a "divine zap" is not the long-range answer.

Being truly spiritual is simply being true to Christ in yielding to Him day by day and moment by moment. It does not all come at once for all of us; it comes in painfully small amounts, a bit at a time. But no matter how it comes, there are no shortcuts to spirituality (MacArthur, Jr., *The Charismatics,* p. 198).

The central passage shedding light on this problem is 1 Corinthians 12:13 where Paul indicates that all believers have been "baptized . . . into one body." And in verse 30 Paul asks the question: "Do all speak in tongues?" It is obviously rhetorical, anticipating a negative response.

What was the significance of tongues in the New Testament?

Most evangelical commentators agree that the primary purpose was to be a *sign.* Both in Acts 2 and in 1 Corinthians 14:22, we see that the sign was to unbelievers to signify the presence and power of God.

At Corinth, however, the gift appears to be used also for purposes of *edification.* The one who spoke in an unknown tongue without interpretation edified himself (14:4), but the one who spoke in the congregation with an unknown tongue and was followed by an interpreter contributed to edifying the congregation (14:5, 26).

Still a third purpose for tongues was in *prayer* (14:2). In a sense this is self-edification. Stedman argues that the use of tongues in congregational meetings was permitted but not originally intended. Perhaps 1 Corinthians 14 indicates that Paul expected the Corinthians to use it in their congregational life and that its benefit was not merely for unbelievers as Stedman intimates (*Body Life,* Regal, p. 47). One does not edify unbelievers, and edification apparently was possible at Corinth if tongues was exercised in the proper way.

Present-day Analysis

With various subcategories and nuances of interpretation and application, it appears that there are generally three categories into which one's analysis of contemporary tongues-speaking must fall.

Obviously one can admit that *a genuine spiritual gift has been restored to the church* in these latter days, again for purposes of sign and edification. One does not have to be enthusiastic about the charismatic movement to agree with Ryrie's caution: "What about tongues today? One cannot say that God would never give this gift or others of the limited gifts today, but everything indicates that the need for the gift ceased with the production of the written Word" (*The Holy Spirit,* Moody, p. 89).

Ryrie's mention of the "production of the written Word" brings up the 1 Corinthians 13:8–10 argument, sometimes called *the perfect thing* or *completed canon* argument. Hocking has no doubt about the meaning: "Tongues come to an abrupt stop when the 'perfect' comes. As a sign gift, they were needed to confirm God's Word until it was completed" (*Spiritual Gifts,* Sounds of Grace Ministries). Ryrie is more cautious.

Some consider that the expression "tongues they will cease" in 1 Corinthians 13:8 (NASB) is a proof that tongues specifically was a limited gift. The argument against such an interpretation is that the passage is contrasting the present state with the external state and therefore is not speaking of the gift of tongues. However, it should be noted that the wider and immediate context is talking about the gift of tongues to a very great extent, and there is no reason not to consider that it is the gift spoken of in this verse. It is also worthy of note that the principal thesis of Chapter 13 is that love never fails, even though tongues and prophecy do and even though the whole present imperfect state fails (*The Holy Spirit,* p. 81).

I am not arguing for open acceptance of the movement, but rather an open-mindedness toward the views of other believers. Scriptures will scarcely support the conclusion that the option of tongues is closed simply because the gift ceased at the end of the first century. Smith's dogmatism is frightening. "When tongues ceased, they ceased. Since the Apostolic Age the Holy Spirit has not and will not again cause people to speak in tongues" (*Tongues in Biblical Perspective,* p. 92).

A second possibility is that tongues-speaking as we know it today is indeed *supernatural in the sense that it is satanic.* Certainly Satan has a reputation as one who seeks to forge his own replicas of what God gives. There is no reason to think he does not have false tongues speakers just as he has had false prophets down through the ages. While recognizing this is a real possibility, the discretion of Gundry is well-taken: "We would prefer to think that such cases are rare and should leave the judgment to God unless the indications are perfectly clear" ("Facing the Issue," *Moody Monthly,* p. 101).

The ready criticism with which some evangelicals attack other believers on this issue reminds one of the Pharisees attributing the work of the Lord to the power of Satan. Though in some cases religious fraud is not only possible but blatant, such verbal denunciation is as dangerous today as it was in the first century (Mark 3:23–30).

A third position gaining popularity is that *tongues-speaking is primarily a psychological experience.* It could be self-induced through the forced repetition of unintelligible expressions or some form of temporary subconscious euphoria which resembles spiritual ecstacy. Quite obviously tongues-speaking could be psychological. When some leaders in the charismatic movement advertise books and tapes which teach persons how to produce nonsense syllables with the intent of learning to speak in tongues, it is easy to see how this explanation could account for a large segment of those engaged in the phenomenon. The possibility of a psychologized state should cause us to be careful in attributing any tongues experience either to the gifts of the Spirit or to the power of Satan.

What Are the Biblical Guidelines?

It would seem that evangelicals who wish to speak in tongues should take every precaution to demonstrate the biblical orientation of their gift. In order to do so, at least four basic guidelines must be employed.

They should openly acknowledge that speaking in tongues does not reflect greater spiritual experience or a higher level of spiritual maturity. In other words, a tongues speaker is not closer to God than one who does not speak in tongues.

They should not seek the gift: not try to "learn how" to speak in tongues or try to teach anyone else to speak in tongues. Certainly we learn *how to use* spiritual gifts such as teaching and evangelism, but that is different from learning *how to get* a spiritual gift. The latter is patently unbiblical because spiritual gifts are given in the sovereignty of the Holy Spirit (1 Cor. 12:7–11).

They should not seek to force this gift on another person.

The gift should be exercised according to these rules outlined in 1 Corinthians 14:
- For edification (v. 26, NASB)
- No more than three should speak (v. 27)
- Never without an interpreter (vv. 27–28)
- Conducted without chaos and confusion (vv. 33, 40)

Some suggest that the church should prohibit women from speaking in tongues in a public service (vv. 34–35). Not all commentators agree that these verses refer to either tongues-speaking or prophecy. They may simply be a criticism of a synagogue "chatter section" which apparently disrupted public worship.

We should *not*:
- Respond with an emotional, experientially-based, negative view of the tongues movement. Some evangelicals criticize the movement for its experience orientation and then attack it on the basis of "what they did to our church."
- Try to disprove tongues by using questionable exegesis.
- Attack the tongues speaker or the charismatic movement in bitterness, strife, or intolerance.
- Make this the big theological issue and try to confront charismatics to provoke debate.

We should:
- Understand what the Bible teaches on the subject by carefully studying passages referring to it.
- Insist that charismatics follow the biblical rules for practicing the gift they claim to have.
- Show love and tolerance in keeping with Paul's suggestion, "Do not forbid speaking in tongues" (1 Cor. 14:39).
- Take precautions against division and schism in our own churches.

It is my opinion that evangelicals have been trying to attack a pragmatic problem by theologizing it out of existence. It has not worked. We can request, and even require, tongues speakers to abide by biblical guidelines or keep private the gift they claim to exercise. Schools have the right to identify certain rules concerning the use of any gift on campus. And in the church we should recognize the necessity of edification and the unity that spiritual gifts should exemplify. A. W. Tozer set a positive example for the Christian and Missionary Alliance denomination when he offered the following four-word motto regarding tongues: "Seek not, forbid not."

In a fine article suggesting a mediating posture such as I have sought, Millard Erickson shares Paul's great concern for understanding and communication.

Whether or not we believe the Holy Spirit is bestowing charismatic gifts such as speaking in tongues today, we can be assured that He is at work filling, sanctifying, empowering and guiding believers, and producing His fruits. In this we can rejoice. And this we ought to seek ("Is Tongues-speaking for Today?" *The Standard,* Nov. 1, 1973, p. 21). I agree.

The Gift of Interpretation
Tongues and interpretation are unique among the spiritual gifts in that the public exercise of one gift is dependent on the public

exercise of the other. Flynn covers all the bases when he says, "The gift of interpretation, when the tongue was a foreign language, would be the ability to translate by someone who did not know the language. In the case of ecstatic utterance, the gift would be to interpret nonlinguistic sounds" (*19 Gifts,* p. 180).

Presumably, if tongues are languages, one could speak in a certain language in public worship having the utterance translated by someone who had learned that language. Orderliness could prevail and edification could result. But that is not exercising the gift of interpretation.

The Greek word in question is *hermeneia,* translated two times in the *New American Standard Bible* and *King James Version* by the word "interpretation" (1 Cor. 12:10; 14:26). The verb form, *diermeneuō,* is more common, appearing six times (Luke 24:27; Acts 9:36; 1 Cor. 12:30; 14:5, 13, 27), and a noun construction meaning "interpreter" is used in 1 Corinthians 14:28 (*diermeneutes*). A closely related term, *hermeneuō,* is used three times by John (1:38, 42; 9:7) and once by the writer of the Book of Hebrews (7:2).

In some references the definition of the various terms is clear: to translate from one language to another such as in Acts 9:36, for example, "a certain disciple named Tabitha (which translated in Greek is called Dorcas)." But in 1 Corinthians 12 and 14 the terms are interwoven with speaking in tongues in such a way as to indicate interpretation as a distinct gift of the Spirit.

We must define interpretation in harmony with understanding tongues. If tongues are translatable languages, then interpretation has to do with giving meaning to the speaker's words in the language common to the gathered group. On the other hand, if tongues are ecstatic utterances and not a language at all, interpretation is, as Lange puts it, "an ability which implied the power of bringing the understanding (*nous*) to bear upon the meaning of the things wrought by the Spirit, and thus to consciously apprehend them" (*A Commentary on the Holy Scriptures,* Zondervan, 20:253).

Discerning What the Spirit Is Saying

In either case, neither the words nor their contexts required an exact word-by-word translation of the message, but rather a revelation by the Holy Spirit displaying the meaning of the utterance. It is important to note that meaning and understanding are key ideas in Paul's treatment of this gift. It is not the *experience* of tongues-speaking which is in focus but rather the *communication* of God-given ideas through interpretation.

In the case of the interpretation of tongues, it would seem that Paul is not thinking of interpretation in the sense of translating one language into another, which would presume that "tongues" had a coherent scheme of grammar, syntax, and vocabulary. Rather, interpretation here seems to be more akin to discerning what the Spirit is saying through the one who is speaking in tongues (Colin Brown, *Dictionary of New Testament Theology,* Vol. 3, p. 1080).

The clear purpose of the gift is to edify the church. That is why the word(s) appear five times in a context which deals with the upbuilding ministry of public worship (1 Cor. 14). Apparently the gift could be given to the same individual who exercised the gift of tongues (v. 13) or to another person in the group (v. 27).

If there is no interpreter present, the tongues speaker must confine himself to private exercise of his gift (v. 28). The Scripture is clear that one who knows he has the gift of tongues should determine in advance of a public meeting whether or not one with the gift of interpretation will be present. Such careful attention to the use of spiritual gifts is essential to the order God wants to maintain in congregational life (vv. 33, 40).

Edification is nurtured in an atmosphere of design and disciplined behavior. Noise and pandemonium distort the attitudes and emotions of worshipers and distract from necessary understanding. The orderliness of Christian worship stood in contrast to first-century paganism. As Robertson notes, "It seems clear that this ecstatic utterance was not uncontrollable; it was very different from the frenzy of some heathen rites, in which the worshiper parted with both reason and power of will" (*The International Critical Commentary, 1 Corinthians,* Scribner's, p. 268). Though order was achieved by limiting the number and succession of speakers, the gift of interpretation was the key to edification.

If a tongues speaker does not have the gift of interpretation, and if an entire congregation is dependent on one interpreter to receive a message from God through tongues, it is a situation fraught with danger. When the pastor preaches, we can check his explanations by comparing them with Scripture and commentaries, but in a tongues message we apparently are at the mercy of the interpreter.

One can see how such a gift can be misused. Smith goes so far as to say:

In every case where a claim to have the gift of interpretation of tongues has been weighed, it has been found wanting. Scientific analysis has pointed out that there is no relationship between the tongues and the supposed interpretation (*Tongues in Biblical,* p. 99).

Though his dogmatism dampens my enthusiasm for his case, Smith points up a danger we must heed. Since interpretation is the key to meaning, it stands in a place of even greater importance than does the gift of tongues, though one without the other is meaningless toward the goal of edification.

It is admittedly difficult to deal with the subjects of this chapter. Yet we must honestly face the realities of 1 Corinthians 14 and the practice and malpractice of the gifts of tongues and interpretation in the first-century church. There is no question that these gifts are abused today, just as there is no question that the gift of evangelism is abused today. Yet Christians must exercise caution and tolerance. Veteran missionary Don Hillis writes,

> The third Person of the Trinity is also the Spirit of unity. It is His nature to love the brethren. It is through Him the love of God is shed abroad in our hearts. Any lack of love on our part for the brethren, any "party" spirit, ("I am of Apollos," etc.), any spirit of divisiveness is not of Him. Any such spirit within us serves to quench the Spirit.
>
> The Children of Israel were accused of limiting "the Holy One of Israel" (Ps. 78:41–42). Nor is the church any less guilty of limiting (quenching) the Person and work of the Holy Spirit. The Spirit of God is "straitened" within us. His ministry is unlimited, unhampered, and unquenched only as we walk in obedience to Him. The fullness of the Spirit is enjoyed by those who are responsive to Him. The liberty of the Holy Spirit to freely direct and control our lives, to fulfill His own wishes, and to do to us and through us all He desires is the need of the hour. *Quench not the Spirit.* There is no gift of the Spirit which can be considered a substitute for the Spirit-controlled life (*Tongues, Healing, and You,* Baker, pp. 38–39).

6
Knowledge and Wisdom

In the rich theology of the Book of Romans, the Apostle Paul "takes a break" from developing doctrine to explain the relationship in God's plan between Israel and the church (chapters 9—11). At the end of the section, he offers a beautiful doxology for either personal edification or corporate worship. It begins with a reference to the knowledge and wisdom of God.

Oh, the depth of the riches of the wisdom and knowledge of God! How unsearchable His judgments, and His paths beyond tracing out! "Who has known the mind of the Lord? Or who has been His counselor?" "Who has ever given to God, that God should repay him?" For from Him and through Him and to Him are all things. To Him be the glory forever! Amen (Rom. 11:33–36).

God's qualities of wisdom and knowledge are reflected in His people through the spiritual gifts of wisdom and knowledge. These gifts are essential for men who serve as elders, but they are frequently found in believers who hold no church office, but who are greatly used by God in family, church, and community to provide a moderating presence which is indeed reflective of God's presence. The gifts are linked in 1 Corinthians 12:8 and both have to do with the mind—a godly understanding which enables individuals and groups of believers to make correct decisions.

The Gift of Knowledge

Some words used to identify spiritual gifts are rare. Terms like *kubernēseis* (administration), for example, must be tracked down in a thorough word study in order to catch nuances of meaning which serve as clues to interpretation.

Gnōsis (knowledge) is one of the more common terms in the New Testament and there is little difficulty in defining it. The hermeneutical trick is to clarify the unique contextual usage in 1 Corinthians 12:8: "to another the message of knowledge by means of the same Spirit." What specifically is the gift of knowledge?

Any attempt at honest exegesis must recognize the relationship between knowledge and wisdom in this verse. It is on this issue that commentators do not agree. Here are some sample explanations:

Lange—"We might take the distinction between these two to be that of theoretical and practical knowledge (*A Commentary on the Holy Scriptures,* Zondervan, 20:251).

Edwards—"Wisdom was the prerogative of the mature Christian; knowledge was available to the immature as well (*A Commentary on the First Epistle to the Corinthians,* Hodder and Stoughton, p. 315).

Beet—"*Knowledge* is mere acquaintance with things past, present, or future. *Wisdom* is, from the Christian point of view, such a direct grasp of underlying principles and eternal realities as enables a man to choose the right goal and the best path in life" (*A Commentary on St. Paul's Epistles to the Corinthians,* Hodder and Stoughton, p. 215).

Godet—"We shall rather see in *gnōsis* a notion of effort, investigation, discovery . . . and in *sophia* (wisdom), on the contrary, the idea of a calm possession of truth already acquired, as well as of its practical applications" (*Commentary on St. Paul's First Epistle to the Corinthians,* T. and T. Clark, 2:195).

John Calvin—"Let us then take *knowledge* as meaning *ordinary information,* and *wisdom* as including revelations that are of a more secret and sublime order" (*Commentaries on the Epistle to the Corinthians,* Calvin Translation Society, 1:40).

We examine this relationship later in the chapter, but there does seem to be an emphasis on wisdom as a deeper and more practical understanding of truth.

What Kind of Knowledge?

First, what kind of knowledge is in view in the spiritual gift of knowledge? Robertson uses the words *insight* and *illumination* to describe the intellectual process involved (*Word Pictures in the New Testament,* Harper, 4:169). The uses of the word in 1 Corinthians indicate that Paul intended to combat a pseudo-spiritual intellectualism in Corinth (8:1–2).

There is also a link between the New Testament concept of *mystery* and the gift of knowledge to understand those mysteries (13:2). Since the revelation of the mysteries was supernatural, the interpretation is also supernatural.

There doubtless was a time in the early days of the church when knowledge was a revelational gift, that is, God gave new truth to unfold His plan to man. But that was before the completion of the canon of Scripture.

Now knowledge seems to be interpretive in function, leading the recipient of the gift into an understanding of God's revealed truth concerning His work in the world (Eph. 3:3–6). Because of this deeper "enlightenment," the gift of knowledge, by its visibility, tends to puff up. Knowledge brings power and with it the temptation to take a superior attitude toward others.

The gift of knowledge is a prime example of how spiritual gifts need to be developed. Godet reminds us that "knowledge advances by means of subjective and deliberate study, which, if it is not to deviate from the straight line of divine truth, must be carried on according to the light of the Spirit" (*Commentary on St. Paul's First Epistle*, 2:196). Perhaps the gift of knowledge is most evident in Christian scholars who research, investigate, interpret, and explain God's special and natural revelation, but there is a practical dimension to the gift as well. Criswell reminds us how the church benefited from the gift of knowledge in the first century, and how it still operates in the church today.

It was with this gift of knowledge that Peter revealed the covetous corruption in the Jerusalem church, recorded in Acts 5:3. It was with this gift of knowledge that John wrote of the Seven Churches of Asia in Revelation 2—3. It is with this gift of knowledge that God's leaders in the churches today come to know in right judgment and appraisal the moral, sound, doctrinal, and organizational situation that blesses the work of the Lord (*The Holy Spirit in Today's World*, Zondervan, p. 173).

A small factory had to stop operations when an essential piece of machinery broke down. When none of the factory personnel could get it operating again, an outside expert was called in. After looking over the situation for a minute, the expert took a hammer and gently tapped the machine on a certain spot, and it immediately started running again. When he submitted his bill for $100, the plant supervisor went into a rage and demanded an itemized bill. It read as follows: "For hitting the machine, $1; for knowing where to hit, $99."

It is axiomatic in today's church that we must have people who "know where to hit." No, they're not fixing the machinery and certainly not physically hitting other believers, but those crucial decisions in business meetings, the courage to carry through on necessary discipline, and the appropriate word of admonition are essential to the biblical operation of today's church.

In my judgment, the ultimate key to understanding the gift of knowledge is found in 1 Corinthians 2:11–16. Here Paul identifies a level of understanding which is beyond the natural man: "The man without the Spirit does not accept the things that come from the Spirit of God, for they are foolishness to him, and he cannot understand them, because they are spiritually discerned" (v. 14).

In an article entitled "Spirituality and Leadership," I attempted to demonstrate how spiritual behavior is related to leadership.

As one studies the various passages of Scripture dealing with *pneumatikos,* he is impressed with the close link between being spiritual and being mature. One almost gets the impression that the new convert, the neophyte in Christian doctrine, cannot be *pneumatikos* simply because he or she has not had time to mature in the faith. By the same token, the use of the word "mature" in this context is closely linked to the role of the Holy Spirit and the Word in the life of the growing Christian (1 Cor. 2:15—3:4).

We hardly have space here to discuss the three types of people implied in the passage. What is important is the utilization of the word *pneumatikos* within the context of nourishment, infancy, childish conflict, and growth. Obviously, the spiritual Christian is one who no longer needs milk because he is growing up in the things of the Lord. He is able to discern all things, or to make intelligent judgments, a clear reference to Spirit-produced wisdom (*Studies in Formative Spirituality,* Vol. 3, Feb. 1982, p. 45).

In context, the Corinthian passage indicates that spiritual truths are also not clearly understood by carnal Christians. Only those who are born of the Spirit can come to grips with biblical interpretation. And apparently there is a level of understanding God's truth which is reserved for those to whom the Holy Spirit has chosen to give the gift of knowledge.

Certainly we would be less than wise to miss the obvious connection among the spiritual gifts which have to do with study and perception: knowledge, wisdom, teaching, prophecy, and possibly administration. Perhaps we need to get a fresh insight into the church's need for knowledge to combat, or at least balance, the surging tide of experiential theology so popular at the end of the 20th century.

The Gift of Wisdom

Wisdom is another limitless theme in Scripture. Several Old Testament books speak about it at great length, and for centuries it has been a significant religious theme in the Middle East. The very essence of wisdom is consistent with the nature of God, and like truth, its source is in the Creator. Furthermore, wisdom is not something which, like doctrine or science, can be taught in a classroom. It is a combined exercise of mind and spirit as a Christian responds to God's guiding and gifting.

Wisdom can be accumulated through experience, but this is not true of the "message of wisdom" which marks the spiritual gift. As with all spiritual gifts, the gift of wisdom is supernatural, focusing on the interpretation of truth, producing solutions to problems, or applying knowledge to spiritual life.

Earlier in the chapter, I attempted to make distinctions between "the message of wisdom" and "the message of knowledge" since their side-by-side appearance in 1 Corinthians 12:8 indicates they are distinct gifts. Edwards seems to think that there is a unique distinction in 1 Corinthians, apart from the use of *sōphia* and *gnōsis* as they appear elsewhere in the New Testament.

Their use in this epistle seems to show that *logos sophias* denotes the power of expounding spiritual truths, which it is the gift of the spiritual man, the *teleios,* both to understand and to speak. Its object is revealed truth; its power is the illumination of the spirit; its method a spiritual synthesis; and its results are communicated to others in words taught by the Holy Ghost (*A Commentary on the First Epistle,* p. 315).

It is significant that both gifts—wisdom and knowledge—are introduced by the phrase, "the word of," implying the practical nature of these spiritual gifts. That is in keeping with what we know about spiritual gifts in general. They are not ethereal or mystical rites practiced only in secret by the initiated, but rather a demonstration of ministry as it serves to edify the church. Godet is most helpful in understanding the relationship between knowledge and wisdom. Says the great Lutheran writer, "Gnōsis makes the teacher; wisdom, the preacher and pastor. When corrupted, the former becomes gnosticism, the speculation of the intellectualist; the latter, dead orthodoxy" (*Commentary on St. Paul's First Epistle,* 2:195–96).

In the Old Testament, wisdom apparently involved the ability to grapple with the problems of life and is seen in principles of ethical behavior in the Wisdom Literature. Though the Greek word appears 75 times throughout the New Testament, the gift is identified only in 1 Corinthians 12:8. This raises the question of the difference between the general references and the specific one. In his book, Rick Yohn speaks to this question in some detail.

But how does the gift differ from the general wisdom available to all believers? Primarily *in the consistency of use and results.* The individual gifted with wisdom will consistently make wise decisions and provide godly insights for problems. The results will be pure, peaceable, gentle, reasonable, full of mercy and good fruits, unwavering, and without hypocrisy.

The person using this gift will soon become known among his associates. He will be the one individuals consult as they face problems. He will be the opinion setter in the church whether he holds an office or not. His opinion will be highly respected (*Discover Your Spiritual Gift and Use It,* Tyndale, p. 96).

Most commentators agree that we should not attach importance to the order in which the spiritual gifts are listed in 1 Corinthians 12:8–10. In view of the prominence of prophecy in chapter 14, for example, why would it be sixth on a list if the order was intended to convey importance and value?

Developing Christian Values

Speaking of value, wisdom certainly is a gift applied in developing a Christian system of values. One commentary suggests that wisdom "is the more comprehensive term. By it we know the true value of things through seeing what they really are; it is spiritual insight and comprehension" (*A Critical and Exegetical Commentary on the First Epistle of Paul to the Corinthians, The International Critical Commentary,* p. 265). Incidentally, there is no definite article in the Greek text, but rather the expression "a word of wisdom." Perhaps there is an emphasis here on communicating God's value system to others. So much of the world's value system permeates what we read, see, and hear that we need those who can give timely words to help us recognize the subtle worldly influences that surround us.

Paul distinguishes between the philosophy of the world and the philosophy of Christ, and indicates that Christians need to learn how to see things from "divine viewpoint" rather than being fogged in by the secularistic materialism and humanism of a pagan culture. Perhaps it is the gift of "a word of wisdom" that enables the Christian to see beyond the smog of earthly intellect to the unique order of priorities in the mind of God. For My thoughts are not your thoughts, neither are your ways My ways, declares the Lord. As the heavens are higher than the earth, so are My ways higher than your ways and My thoughts than your thoughts (Isa. 55:8–9).

7
Pastoring and Teaching

How often it is said of God's servant in a local church, "He is a fine pastor, but not a good preacher." Or perhaps it is the reverse: "His preaching is wonderful, but he's not really a shepherd to the flock." Maybe it is the linking of pulpit teaching with shepherding the flock, along with the complicated grammar of Ephesians 4, which leads many to see pastor-teacher as one gift rather than two. Gene Getz writes:

Pastors or shepherds were those who gave special help to new churches. They were also *teachers* that helped both in the organization of the church as well as in its growth through the process of instruction. In the first-century church they seemingly had a foundational ministry, along with the others who had the greater gifts. They went from church to church assisting in the appointment of local leadership, and making sure the church learned the basic doctrines of Christianity (*Sharpening the Focus of the Church*, Moody Press, p. 101).

There is no question that pastors are required to teach, and it is possible that one who holds the office of shepherd should also have the gift of teaching, though the New Testament is not conclusive on the subject. On one hand, we may not be under any exegetical demand to tie the two together. On the other hand, there are some mutual responsibilities. Foulkes puts it this way:

Apostles and evangelists had a particular task in planting the church in every place; prophets, for bringing a particular word from God to a situation. Pastors and teachers were gifted to be responsible for the day-to-day building up of the church. There is no hard and fast line to be drawn between the two (*The Epistle of Paul to the Ephesians,* Eerdmans, p. 119).

Though teaching is linked with pastoring in one way or another, the work of the shepherd more directly involves leading, protecting, caring for, and feeding the flock of God in broad and general ways, therefore, I will treat the gifts separately.

The Gift of Pastoring

The church is the ongoing work of Jesus Christ in the world. As such, its use of spiritual gifts is reflective of our Lord's own earthly ministry. No doubt He possessed every spiritual gift in its most perfect form, though we do not have a record of His exercising them all. Some of the gifts are uniquely reminiscent of the Incarnate Word—teaching, prophesying, showing mercy, and certainly shepherding (John 10; Heb. 13:20; 1 Peter 2:25).

The Greek word from which a pastor-shepherd ministry comes is *poimen,* whose root meaning denotes protection and care. We call the shepherd of a church "pastor" from the Latin translation of *poimen* (*pastores*). Only in Ephesians 4:11 are congregational leaders called shepherds, though the idea of the shepherd-leader in the church appears frequently in the New Testament (John 21:16; Acts 20:28; 1 Peter 5:2).

In focusing on Ephesians 4:11, we see again the need for distinguishing between gifts and offices. The five items identified in this verse describe gifted leaders, already given gifts by the Spirit, and now given to the church by Christ. In each case an office as well as a gift seems to be implied. With the office of pastor comes accompanying authority and responsibility in the congregation, but not to the point of autocracy, as Peter clearly warns (1 Peter 5:1–4).

The very analogy of one who cares for sheep helps us to understand the multiple facets of this gift. The pastor is to guard the flock from its enemies to preserve it from destruction from within and without. The protecting function of a shepherd is only part of the task. He must also teach, lead, feed, and prepare refreshing rest for his charges. It is also his responsibility to seek the lost, redirect the straying, heal the wounds of the injured, and unify the flock.

Far from creating a dependence on himself, the pastor's duty is to lead the flock to ministry (Eph. 4:12), to equip them to serve Christ by serving each other, and to build a capacity for preserving and edifying the local church.

Note that the first three gifts listed in verse 11 refer more to the universal church and the last two to the local church as we know it. This is not to say that such a specific division was clear in the first century, but rather that it has evolved in later years of the church. Lange points out:

Little good has ever resulted from the attempt to reproduce accurate as *jure divirio* those distinctions which expositors discover in the offices of the primitive church. It may be remarked that while this phrase shows that every pastor ought to be a teacher, putting the former phase of duty first, it will ever be the case that through native endowment some ministers are better adapted for one part of the duty than for the other, though there is no warrant for total neglect of either ("Ephesians," *A Commentary on the Holy Scriptures,* Vol. 21, p. 150).

The gift of pastoral care is a ministry to people beyond the level of teaching them. It implies a dimension of patience, an attitude of long-suffering not essential to the ministry of teaching in a noncongregational setting, for example. To be sure, there is an element of pastoring in teaching, and the teacher who applies this element in the Spirit greatly enhances his ministry.

It is encouraging to see the gift of pastoral ministry being developed with enthusiasm again in today's church. In the late 1960s the church experienced a low in self-concept. The constant attacks of that decade took their toll, and discouragement was rampant. Veteran pastors seem more optimistic regarding what Christ is doing in His church. Potential pastors are attending evangelical seminaries at a rate unprecedented in the modern era.

Seminary students today are anxious for the people-developing type of ministry which biblical pastoring calls for. David Mains reflected during his pastoral days:

It is no longer enough for me, as a pastor, to feel satisfied with a solitary display of my gift. My ministry must include assisting each one in our congregation to find expression for his particular gift or gifts (*Full Circle,* Word, p. 68).

Equipping the Flock

Perhaps we should notice that the gift of shepherding is not necessarily locked into the office of pastoring. The beautiful Parable of Jesus recorded in John 10 suggests four interpretations and applications:

- A literal shepherd and literal sheep.
- Christ, the shepherd, and believers as His sheep.
- The local church shepherd and the congregation.

- A believer of spiritual maturity shepherding fellow believers of lesser maturity.

Any pastor who understands the latter application will be thrilled to have as many auxiliary shepherds as possible in his congregation.

Pastor Les Flynn tells the story of Paul Rader's multiplying ministry at Moody Church in Chicago:

One day Rader challenged a young convert to help with junior boys.

The young man replied, "But I'm in engineering and work some Sundays."

Rader retorted, "Why don't you quit that job? You pray about it and I'll pray too."

Within a week the young man was offered the position of manager of the Tabernacle Publishing Company. The jump from engineering to publishing started a series of events which ultimately led to the establishment of a large and influential Christian publishing house. The young man and his wife were Drs. Victor and Bernice Cory, founders of Scripture Press.

Others influenced in their Christian ministry through the shepherding gift of Rader were Dr. V. R. Edman, who became president of Wheaton College; Dr. Howard Ferrin, who presided over Providence Bible Institute and later became chancellor of Barrington College; and Merrill Dunlap, well known Gospel song composer, to name just a few (*19 Gifts of the Spirit,* Victor, pp. 72–73).

In addition to whatever else it may be, the gift of pastoring is a catalyst geared to release the gift potential of those in the flock. It also could be that the Holy Spirit, knowing the vast and diverse tasks of congregational care, equips pastors with several gifts to enable them to minister effectively as the shepherds of Christ's flock.

The Gift of Teaching

Just as the gift of pastoring reminds us of the earthly shepherding ministry of the Lord Jesus, so an appreciation of the gift of teaching should lead us to think about Jesus as the master teacher.

One who exercises the gift of teaching in the church follows the pattern of Christ feeding His church. In looking at the spiritual gifts, it is more difficult to understand the relationship of some than others to the collective body of Christ, though I have tried to show that relationship in dealing with each gift. The communal context for the exercise of gifts is basic, and one can certainly see how the gift of teaching is of significant importance in the total role of edifying the church, which is the ultimate goal of all gifts.

Howard A. Snyder warns against "the tendency to over-individualize spiritual gifts" when he says:

Western Christianity in general has tended to over-individualize the Gospel to the detriment of its more communal and collective aspects, and contemporary conceptions of spiritual gifts have suffered from this tendency. Spiritual gifts are too often thought of as strictly a matter of one's "private" relationship to God, without regard for the Christian community. In contrast, Paul repeatedly emphasizes that the Spirit's gifts are for the edification of the church, and that they lose their significance if this emphasis is lost ("Misunderstanding Spiritual Gifts," *Christianity Today,* Oct. 12, 1973, pp. 15–16).

The gift of teaching is mentioned in three of the four major passages dealing with spiritual gifts (Rom. 12:7; 1 Cor. 12:28–29; Eph. 4:11). In the Romans passage Paul emphasizes that the one who teaches must see his gift as a service to the community and must exercise it in relation to those who make up the body. The same kind of communal emphasis appears in 1 Corinthians

12, especially since the reference to "teachers" appears after the long section dealing with unity-in-diversity which is the body of Christ. In the Ephesians passage, the context again is clearly the church, both universal (as the earlier verses of the chapter clearly specify) and local, in view of the fact that this epistle is being written to a local church at Ephesus.

However, the Ephesians passage also implies a sense of office since the word *didaskaloi* appears in line with the other offices mentioned in the verse. As I mentioned earlier, the concept of "pastors and teachers" (v. 11) can be understood either as two separate offices or as a description of "pastors who teach." Whichever interpretation we prefer, we cannot escape the fact that in the other two passages teaching is clearly a distinct gift from pastoring.

MacPherson treats the Ephesians passage in an interesting way and draws a distinction I have not seen discussed in any other place. After indicating that the teacher is one who has been charged with the task of "imparting doctrinal instruction," he goes on to suggest that this office

is the Christian equivalent of the Jewish "rabbi." The work of the pastor was to follow up in his own more limited sphere that of the apostle; the work of the teacher was to follow up in a systematic way the work of the prophet. "If the prophet," says Godet on 1 Corinthians 12:28, "may be compared to the traveler who discovers new countries, the teacher is like the geographer who combines the scattered results of these discoveries and gives a methodological statement of them (*Commentary on St. Paul's Epistle to the Ephesians,* T. and T. Clark, p. 311).

The concept of the *didaskalos* (teacher) is a common but important one in the New Testament. Kittel tells us that it occurs 58 times, 48 of which are in the Gospels. Of those in the Gospels, the word refers to Jesus 41 times and to others only

7 times. (*Theological Dictionary of the New Testament,* Eerdmans, 2:152). The Apostle Paul applied the term to himself in 1 Timothy 2:7 and 2 Timothy 1:11. Of course these are only references to the noun form, and do not include the many other references to the process of teaching.

Explaining God's Written Revelation

I have attempted to make a distinction between the prophet in Old Testament times and in New Testament times, and in the use of the gift of prophecy in the church today. It is clear that both Old Testament prophets and, to a lesser extent, New Testament prophets engaged in a revelational ministry. That is, they communicated direct truth from God, revealed to them in lieu of written revelation on the subject. As I see it, modern-day exercise of the gift of prophecy is not to communicate new revelation. Rather it is to explain God's written revelation and how to apply it in life.

In contrast, the gift of teaching seems to have always been that of explaining God's truth and how to apply it. The rabbis based their teaching both on the Old Testament Scriptures and on the Talmud and Mishna. New Testament teachers obviously explained the Messianic character of the Old Testament with particular application to Jesus of Nazareth. Today the gift of teaching is much the same as it always has been among God's people. It focuses on written revelation and seeks to show how that revelation is understandable and relevant in any given age. It would seem that the major difference between the gift of teaching in the New Testament church and the gift of teaching today is that the teacher today has the completed canon of Scripture and 19 centuries of church history to shed light on his hermeneutical task. There is a clear implication of study, mental and verbal skills, and reliance on the Holy Spirit in the ministry of teaching.

Jesus promised the disciples that when the Spirit came to them He would guide them into all truth. "He will not speak on His own; He will speak only what He hears, and He will tell you what is yet to come" (John 16:13). A reference to their recording of the New Testament Scriptures? Yes, that surely was included. But limiting that promise only to the inspiration of the New Testament text seems to me to do damage to the phrase "into all truth." Surely the principle of the Spirit's guidance in teaching can be claimed by any Sunday School teacher or pastor in our day just as it was claimed by the men who wrote the New Testament canon. I like the way W. G. T. Shedd suggests that the gift of teaching implies "the common knowledge of a devout and disciplined Christian mind" (*Commentary on Romans,* Scribner's, p. 364).

Teaching was foundational to the church in the New Testament. When believers formed the church at Antioch, Barnabas was sent to minister among them. According to the text of Scripture, "he was a good man, full of the Holy Spirit and faith, and a great number of people were brought to the Lord" (Acts 11:24). But something was still missing. In-depth explanation, interpretation and application of the inspired text of the Old Testament to the lives of believers of the New Testament was needed. So "Barnabas went to Tarsus to look for Saul, and when he found him, he brought him to Antioch. For a whole year Barnabas and Saul met with the church and taught great numbers of people. The disciples were first called Christians at Antioch" (vv. 25–26).

To the Ephesian elders at Miletus Paul says, "You know that I have not hesitated to preach anything that would be helpful to you but have taught you publicly and from house to house" (Acts 20:20).

Every evangelical church is committed to teaching in some form. Though a few churches have experimented with substitutes, the traditional Sunday School is still popular among evangelicals, and there are indications that it may rebound from a downward trend seen at the end of the last decade. Consequently we do well to focus again on the teaching ministry of the church. Rather than just trying to "fill jobs" in the Sunday School with any warm and willing bodies, church leaders should examine people's spiritual gifts and staff Sunday Schools with those who have the gift of teaching.

However, not every Sunday School teacher has the gift of teaching. Since all Christians have some responsibility for sharing their faith and for teaching others, they may be doing so in the same arenas as those who have the gifts of evangelism and/or teaching.

Nevertheless, we need to identify those believers among us whom the Holy Spirit has chosen to equip with the gift of teaching and press them into service. Robertson and Plummer speak to the distinction between general teaching and gift teaching in a very helpful paragraph from their commentary on 1 Corinthians:

It is evident from "Are all teachers?" (12:29) that there was a class of teachers to which only some Christians belonged, and the questions which follow show that "teachers," like "workers of miracles," were distinguished by the possession of some gift. In Ephesians 4:11 we are not sure whether "pastors and teachers" means one class or two, but at any rate, it is probably that whereas "apostles," "prophets," and "evangelists" instructed both the converted and the unconverted, "pastors and teachers" ministered to settled congregations (*A Critical and Exegetical Commentary on the First Epistle of Paul to the Corinthians,* The International Critical Commentary, pp. 279–80).

A further note is found in the Epistle of James where we read that one can choose whether or not he wants to be a teacher, and every Christian ought to be careful about selecting a position of this importance (3:1). In an effort to be consistent with other New Testament passages, we have to recognize that such a personal choice would be based on a person's awareness of having the gift of teaching. When one recognizes that he has that gift, he is responsible for thanking God for it, for seeking to develop it, and for using it to edify the body.

Dr. Roy Zuck points out that there are only three reasons for poor teaching in the church: "If teachers are ineffective, either they do not have the teaching gift, are not developing it, or are not in fellowship with the Lord" (*The Holy Spirit in Your Teaching,* Scripture Press, p. 74).

8
Faith and Giving

Perhaps the most well-known linking of the gifts of faith and giving appears in the first paragraph of the popular love chapter.

If I speak in the tongues of men and of angels, but have not love, I am only a resounding gong or a clanging cymbal. If I have the gift of prophecy and can fathom all mysteries and all knowledge, and if I have a faith that can move mountains, but have not love, I am nothing. If I give all I possess to the poor and surrender my body to the flames, but have not love, I gain nothing (1 Cor. 13:1–3).

To be sure, there is no specific notation that one must give in faith or demonstrate faith by giving, but the dominance of love in exercising spiritual gifts is reflected in both faith and giving.

The Gift of Faith
Since by God's grace every Christian has exercised faith in Christ's finished work in order to become a member of the

family of God, some find it difficult to see how faith can be a special gift—an endowment for ministry in the church. Though the word is the same (*pistis*), the context of 1 Corinthians 12:9, 13:2, and Romans 12:6 demands an interpretation that is consistent with our understanding of the nature of spiritual gifts. The gift of faith is not to be equated with the fruit of faith described in Galatians 5:22. A. T. Robertson well says of 1 Corinthians 12:9, "Not faith of surrender, saving faith, but wonder-working faith" (*Word Pictures in the New Testament*, Harper, 4:169).

The term *wonder-working* may be a bit misleading. This faith does not *produce* the work of God but rather *sets the climate* in which God chooses to unleash *His* miracle-working power. Such faith is neither blind nor irrational. It does not drift aimlessly in search of a destination. Rather, like a piece of steel to a compelling magnet, it attaches itself to the Sovereign of the universe.

The person who demonstrates the gift of faith is characterized by utter dependence on the Lord. He puts little stock in human resources; and even when they are available, he realizes that God has indirectly supplied them through the human donor. The Christian with the gift of faith is able to see what others cannot see, to endure what others cannot endure, and to genuinely trust God when there seems to be no human or natural basis for that trust.

Biblical Examples of Faith

The Bible abounds with examples of this kind of faith, and a tribute to some is written in Hebrews 11. Consider:

Abel and his sacrifice
Noah and his unorthodox carpentry
Abraham looking at Isaac on the altar
Moses and his vision of freedom

Joshua and his commitment to victory

David and his assurance that God would give him the kingdom

Such faith was also demonstrated in the days of the New Testament.

Daily, John the Baptist scanned the burning sand for the promised Messiah.

Twelve men gave up their jobs and homes to follow an itinerant Teacher.

Barnabas gave everything he had to the fledgling church.

Paul and Silas sang praises in a Philippian jail.

Thousands of early Christians looked to God to sustain them in their pagan surroundings.

John wrote his vision of an eternal city which would someday house all who love God.

What does the spiritual gift of faith mean to the church today? Precisely the same dynamic for growth which it has always signified! Building programs need to be started, workers equipped, educational programs sustained, missionaries sent, colleges and seminaries supported, and saints stirred. To some among us the Holy Spirit gives the gift of faith. These gifted men and women become our visionaries. They see beyond the current crop of problems and are not stymied by the "seven last words of the church" ("We've never done it that way before"). Their assurance that God *will* come through for His people is sometimes frustrating to others who want to be more practical and realistic. But Christ, the Lord of the church, knows that progress is dependent on faith leadership.

Though the gift of faith is not to be confused with the act of faith which leads to regeneration, there is a sense in which they are related because each depends on the response of God.

When J. A. Clarke was translating the New Testament into Luba Katanga, he searched for a way to communicate the dynamic biblical concept of faith, a word used in various forms over 500 times in the Scripture. While journeying through mountainous terrain, he called his party to a halt so the porters could rest. During the recess, one of them picked up a stone and threw it. It ricocheted down the mountainside into a ravine below, finally splashing in the depths of a river. The sound came back up the mountainside, followed by a fainter echo. As the echo died away the porter turned and said to Clarke, "Twi tabilo." The man was simply saying, "Listen to it," but soon "Twi tabilo" was used to translate the concept of biblical faith— the echo of God's voice from the depths of human hearts; man's response to what God has already provided.

In church administration, the gift of faith is not to be equated with deficit financing. Mortgage programs are not wrong, and indeed are often necessary, but sometimes we over-extend God's credit without asking Him, then call it faith when, in desperation, we call on Him to redeem His good reputation.

A primary characteristic of faith, and all spiritual gifts, is supernatural origin. We should not confuse our general ability to believe God's Word with a unique assurance that something which we believe to be in God's plan will definitely come to pass. There is an important difference here between *assenting* faith and *appropriating* faith.

Appropriating faith is never the result of human ability or strength. We cannot generate it by our own wills, no matter how desperately we attempt to conjure it up. Spiritual gifts are given sovereignly. Though it is biblical to pray for the gift of faith, we are not to demand that God succumb to our analysis of what gifts we need and what we think we can best use. The embarrassed disciples learned this lesson when their best healing efforts counted for nothing on an epileptic boy (Matt. 17:14–21).

In these last decades of the 20th century, we live in an era of unprecedented self-dependence. Man and his machines bow together at the shrine of science, confident that nothing is impossible. The spirit of the age revolts against a supernaturalism which looks to heaven expecting divine intervention on behalf of the people of God.

But perhaps, after years of human effort, the church is ready to recognize itself as the unique possession of a unique God. Perhaps men and women with the gift of faith can lead us in "looking to Jesus" as did the faith heroes recorded in Hebrews 11. Perhaps even in our affluence and materialism, the vitality of Judson and Mueller can live again.

The Gift of Giving

The gifts of faith and giving come together most directly at the point of material support for the work of the church. Practical Christianity could hardly be more poignant in these times of economic difficulty. The grammatical meaning of *hometadidous* is sharing or imparting, and only two of its five biblical appearances are in distinctly "gift-oriented" passages (Luke 3:11; Rom. 1:11; 12:8; Eph. 4:28; 1 Thes. 2:8). Hocking describes the gift as "the ability to give your material goods and financial resources with joy and eagerness, without any motives that would benefit you. . . . It is to be done with the single motive of sharing your wealth with others to the glory of God" (*Spiritual Gifts,* Sounds of Grace Ministries).

That is not to say that the gift of giving concerns itself only, or even primarily, with money. R. C. H. Lenski takes the key passage (Rom. 12:8) to be a "reference to spiritual impartation" as the word is used in Romans 1:11 and 1 Thessalonians 2:8 (*The Interpretation of St. Paul's Epistle to the Romans,* Wartburg, p. 764). No doubt giving one's spiritual resources is a significant part of mutually edifying the body, but evidence is ample for taking the reference here to apply to distributing

one's wealth to others in the name of Christ and for the sake
of His church.

To put it simply then, the one who has the gift of giving
donates generously of his resources to others and does it cheer-
fully because it is a gift and not a duty. We tend to refer such
a gift to the few wealthy among us, but God's work has always
been primarily supported by those of modest means.

To be sure, we welcome the gifts of the wealthy and are
delighted when a millionaire recognizes the gift of giving in
response to a fund drive or a less publicized need, but let us
honestly recognize that in the sovereignty of the Holy Spirit,
the middle- or lower-income Christian also may have the gift of
giving.

It is important to remember that the basic context for the use
of spiritual gifts is the local church. Sometimes believers give
to every cause, social and religious, while allowing the home
congregation to stagger along under the burden of inadequate
finances. Griffith Thomas reminds us that the giver "is to do it
with liberality, communicating freely of his own possessions for
the good of the community" (*Romans—A Devotional Commentary,* Religious Tract Society, p. 26).

Sharing Resources

Two characteristics of a person who has the gift of giving are:
he has resources; he delights in sharing those resources. We
tend to focus on the more glamorous or controversial gifts, but
where would our pastors and teachers be without the support
of those who properly employ the gift of giving?

If it is possible to request a gift from God (as I have previously suggested), then those who ask God to prosper their business
ventures and investments in order that they may give more to
the Lord's work are opting for a biblical pattern. Attitude is as
important as ability in exercising any spiritual gift, however.

The person who writes a check for half a million dollars to Alpha and Omega Christian College in order to get his name on a plaque, a seat on the board, or prestige in the church is not exercising the spiritual gift of giving. (Of course that does not mean Alpha and Omega will turn down the money.)

The word *haplotēs,* rendered "simplicity" in the *King James Version,* is of crucial importance here. The word is translated as "liberality" or "cheerfulness," but the underlying meaning is "joyful eagerness." How many Christians give to God's work with a "joyful eagerness"? Such an attitude is obviously and significantly different from "devoted duty" or even "loyalty to the church." Godet offers a helpful discussion of the word *haplotēs.*

According to its etymological meaning, the word signifies the disposition not to turn back on oneself; and it is obvious that from this first meaning there may follow either that of *generosity,* when man gives without letting himself be arrested by any selfish calculations, or that of *simplicity,* when he gives without his left hand knowing what his right does—that is to say without any vain going back on himself, and without any air of haughtiness (*Commentary on the Epistle to the Romans,* Zondervan, pp. 432–33).

With the exception of one use by James (1:5), *haplotēs* is a Pauline term. The apostle uses it seven times in addition to the Romans 12:8 text. Five of the seven references are in 2 Corinthians, and three of them clearly refer to money.

Some suggest that the key scriptural teaching on the subject of giving is in 2 Corinthians 9 where the central principle appears in verse 6: "Remember this: whoever sows sparingly will also reap sparingly, and whoever sows generously will also reap generously." No compromise, no compulsion, and no complaining, for biblical giving truly reflects the believer's heart attitude and has the glorious result of making him dependent on the

Lord (vv. 8–9). As the giving increases, so also does receiving from the Lord.

Whereas this passage speaks of giving in general terms and aims its message at all believers, the principles and the process are magnified among those who have the gift of giving.

This spiritual attitude toward giving reminds us of the teaching of Christ. He admonished, "When you give to the needy, do not let your left hand know what your right hand is doing, so that your giving may be in secret. Then your Father, who sees what is done in secret, will reward you" (Matt. 6:3–4). An attitude of humility and grace, rather than pride and legalism, should characterize our giving. Giving with pretension and public clamor is an act of hypocrisy, not exercising a spiritual gift.

One more thought. If we can ask people to exercise other spiritual gifts for the benefit of the church, why are we so hesitant and apologetic about asking people to practice the gift of giving? Shouldn't we provide a way in which God's people can develop this spiritual gift? We conduct leadership training sessions for teachers and pastors, but tend to view discussing the use of money as somewhat carnal.

Perhaps we labor under the often-misquoted version of a famous statement: "Money is the root of all evil." But that is not what Paul said. He warned Timothy, "The *love* of money is the root of all evil" (1 Tim. 6:10, KJV), thereby emphasizing again that, in giving, the attitude is more important than the act.

Let us rally to the Cross those who have this necessary spiritual gift. Let us show them that it is not carnal but spiritual to recognize and use their gifts. And while we're at it, let us examine ourselves to see if the Spirit may have given us the gift of giving.

9
Ministering and Discernment

About 35 miles from Jerusalem, on the coastline where Palestine meets the Mediterranean Sea, stands the modern city of Tel Aviv. The port section of the city, called Yafo, is usually referred to as Joppa in the Bible. For centuries it has been a major seaport and was famous during Solomon's reign as the landing place for the cedars of Lebanon, which were floated down and taken ashore for the building of the temple. Joppa was the port from which Jonah sailed in an attempt to run away from God to the city of Tarshish.

New Testament references to the city appear in Acts 9—11, where we read about a woman who lived there during the earliest days of the New Testament church. Luke tells us that "this woman was full of good works and almsdeeds which she did" (Acts 9:36). She ministered from her home. Colossians 3:23 reminds us that we should do everything as unto the Lord, and Dorcas is a New Testament model of such commitment and service. She helped people who were not being helped by others. In Acts 9:39 the weeping women are referred to as "all the widows," which leads us to conclude that Dorcas had a regular ministry with women, particularly those whose husbands had died. Possibly she cared for older women who were not able to care for themselves.

Dorcas had the gift of ministering or "helps," a delightful gift which ought to be more highly recognized in the church today.

The gift of discernment is different, though like ministering, it is an unheralded gift. In the United States House of Representatives there is that trophy of bureaucracy, the Committee on Committees. Presumably its purpose is to coordinate and regulate the membership, activities, and multiple committee functions of the parent body.

In a similar way, the gift of discernment might be called a "gift on gifts." Robertson says that it is given "to tell whether the gifts were really of the Holy Spirit and supernatural" (*Word Pictures in the New Testament,* Harper, 4:169). If there was no gift of discernment available in the theological miasma of the late 20th century, God would have to invent one to help us find our way in the fog.

The Gift of Ministering

A few years ago I was sitting at the front of our church with the other deacons, waiting for a young couple to come forward and be welcomed into membership. As the pastor called their names and they stood, a woman seated across the aisle and three or four rows ahead of them, left her seat. She walked over to the couple, took their infant daughter from the mother, and cared for her in the lobby while the parents came to the front.

A small act of a modern-day Dorcas, to be sure, but typical of this woman's service to the congregation and representative of the gift of ministering—or helps. Expressed in many ways, this gift is plasma to the lifeblood of our churches.

Two words in the original text of Scripture refer to the gift of ministering: *diakonia* in Romans 12:7 and *antilempsis* in 1 Corinthians 12:28. Because different Greek terms are used, it is tempting to wonder whether two separate gifts might be in view. The proximity of the words to the other terms for gifts in both passages, however, and their similar definitions, seem to focus on one gift.

Kittel suggests that *antilempsis* is an obvious reference "to the activity of love in the dealings of the community" (*Theological Dictionary of the New Testament*, Eerdmans, 1:376). And of *diakonia* he writes, [it is] "any discharge of service in genuine love" (*Theological Dictionary*, 2:87). Hocking sees the two as separate gifts and defines the "gift of serving" as "the ability to perform any task or responsibility with joy which benefits others and meets practical and material needs that exist." Of the gift of helps he writes, "The motivation appears to be a desire to help someone else, especially to relieve them of heavy burdens and responsibilities. The 'help' given could be in financial support (Acts 20:35) or organizational responsibilities (Ex. 18:22), or any area which brings support to someone else" (*Spiritual Gifts*, Sounds of Grace Ministries).

The term *diakonia* is broad in scope and we have been wrong to limit it only to pastors and to speak of "entering the ministry" as a narrow occupational choice for very few Christians. Certainly pastors are "ministers." So are deacons and elders, teachers and superintendents, choir members and ushers, visitors and youth directors, nursery helpers and custodians.

The first deacons got their name from the word *diakonia* and their tasks were to minister at tables while the apostles ministered in teaching. We might say both groups of men were engaged in "food service."

This gift of ministering, or helps, represents the "cocoon" in which all the other more specialized gifts are contained. Jesus told His disciples that this is the very essence of New Testament leadership: "The greatest among you should be like the youngest, and the one who rules like the one who serves. . . . I am among you as One who serves" (Luke 22:26–27).

We know that ministering is the work of all the saints because God says so (Eph. 4:12). The church officers mentioned (v. 11) have as their task equipping believers in order that they may minister.

The noun form, *antilempsis,* appears only here and comes from the verb *antilambanesthai* which, in the middle voice, means "to take a burden on oneself." It is so used in Romans 8:26: "the Spirit helps us in our weakness," and in Acts 20:35: "by this kind of hard work we must help the weak." There is no office or authority in view and no permanence to the particular act of helping. Very few cults grow up around people who exercise the gift of helps.

Calvin repudiates this general view and prefers to think of *antilempsis* as "an office, as well as gift, that was exercised in ancient times but of which we have at this day no knowledge whatever" (*Commentaries on the Epistles of Paul the Apostle to the Corinthians,* Calvin Translation Society, 1:416).

Other commentators refer the gift of ministering to a specific office (perhaps that of deacon) because *diakonia* appears in the list of Romans 12 in a somewhat formal way. Shedd abruptly states that the meaning is to be taken "in the restricted sense of the diaconate [because] the writer is enumerating particular gifts and offices in the church" (*Commentary on Romans,* Scribner's p. 364). I see no basis for an office of giving or showing mercy as these gifts are mentioned in verse 8. We need to guard against our Western cultural tendency to fit everything into a formal bureaucratic pattern.

In comparing and uniting the various services indicated by the two terms, we see the scope of church ministry:

Helping the weak - (Acts 20:35)
Slaves serving Christian owners - (1 Tim. 6:2)
General assistance in ministry - (Rom. 16:3, 9)
Teaching and edifying the church - (Eph. 4:12)
Caring for food needs of widows - (Acts 6:1–6)
Sending an offering to other Christians -
    (Rom. 15:26–33)
Serving tables - (Luke 22:27)
Communicating the Gospel to the lost - (2 Cor. 4:1–6)
Serving a guest in your home - (Luke 10:40)

This concept of Christian service as ministering to other people appears in all four of the major listings of spiritual gifts (Rom. 12, 1 Cor. 12, Eph. 4, and 1 Peter 4). In 1 Peter 4 it is beautifully direct: "Minister [your gifts] one to another, as good stewards of the manifold grace of God" (v. 10, KJV). Cranfield talks about the gift of ministering as "the spiritual capacity for practical service" and says that believers should "give themselves wholeheartedly to the fulfillment of the tasks to which their particular endowment is also their divine vocation" (*A Commentary on the Holy Scriptures,* Oliver and Boyd, p. 32).

Perhaps the secret of ministry to others is found in the very wording of Romans 12:7. There is no verb in the Greek text, and in the *King James Version* words have been supplied to support the emphasis: "Ministry . . . ministering." The idea seems to be, "Don't talk about it, do it." And perhaps those who possess this gift are marked by a less-talk-more-action style of service to others and, at the same time, to Christ.

The Gift of Discernment

Shortly after the end of the second missionary journey, possibly in the year A.D. 52, excitement erupted in the synagogue at Ephesus. A traveling evangelist by the name of Apollos came to teach the Scriptures. According to Luke, "He was a learned man, with a thorough knowledge of the Scriptures. He had been instructed in the way of the Lord, and he spoke with great fervor and taught about Jesus accurately, though he knew only the baptism of John" (Acts 18:24–25). Sitting in that assembly were two believers, the beautiful biblical couple we know as Priscilla and Aquila. The sermon didn't sound quite right. What Apollos said was fine: it was what he didn't say that bothered them. The exposition was inadequate. They demonstrated the gift of discernment, though it has nothing to do in this instance with evil spirits or cultic doctrine. Apollos needed more teaching. To meet his need, they invited him home for dinner and explained to him more completely the way of God.

The noun form used in 1 Corinthians 12:10: ("the ability to distinguish between spirits") is *diakrisis*—from *diakrinō,* meaning to judge or evaluate. This gift is closely linked with that of prophecy both here and in 14:29, though it can be seen in all gifts of public ministry. Elsewhere in the New Testament the early church leaders call for discernment on the part of God's people without naming it as a gift (1 Thes. 5:21; 1 John 4:1).

More is involved in the gift of discernment than the serious scriptural comparison for which Luke commended the Bereans, as noble and necessary as that is (Acts 17:10–11). As a divinely given spiritual gift, discernment enables one to intuitively identify truth from error because he has been provided with supernatural analysis. Tongues must be interpreted; prophecy must be discerned. Today, as in the first century, false prophets abound, even within the broad fences of Christendom. Every believer must test the written and spoken words of religious leaders by God's Word. Some, however, possess a special "power of discerning between the true and the false spirit . . . a faculty to apply the test" (*A Commentary on the First Epistle to the Corinthians,* Hodder and Stoughton, p. 318).

The frightening phenomenon of fascination with witchcraft

and the occult in our day calls new attention to the gift of discernment. Once confined to storefront churches in San Francisco, the occult has now "gone respectable." Endor is emerging on college and university campuses from coast to coast, filling classrooms with entranced followers or curious skeptics. *Newsweek* reports, "Courses in a wide variety of occult subjects are now among the most popular additions to the curriculum at many schools" (*Newsweek,* Apr. 9, 1973, p. 41).

Is Western culture interested in the supernatural? There is no doubt about it. The hard shell of secular humanism with its glorification of rational intellect and cold reasoning cannot contain the inner fascination for the metaphysical. Entertainment and book sections of newspapers and magazines reflect national interest in the spirit world. The church needs the gift of discernment. Les Flynn writes,

When a Christian is faced with the supernatural, he is not to mistakenly identify the supernatural with the divine and thus uncritically accept all spirits. Nor is he to be overcritical lest he despise prophesying and quench the Spirit (1 Thes. 5:19–20). The late Dr. Will H. Houghton, when president of Moody Bible Institute, was approached by a woman who was linked with a false cult which claimed inspiration from the spirit world. When he said he couldn't go along with her belief, she replied that he should trust the spirits. Suddenly this verse came to Dr. Houghton's mind: "Beloved, believe not every spirit, but try the spirits whether they are of God: because many false prophets are gone out into the world" (1 John 4:1, KJV). The claim to have the key to the Scriptures, to possess divine utterances, to have spiritual power is not to be trusted but tested (*19 Gifts of the Spirit,* Victor, pp. 152–53).

We see, then, that testing and evaluating spirits to determine whether they are of God or of Satan, particularly with respect to prophecy, is one use of discernment. Other uses in the church are:

• An awareness, most likely through inner witness of the Spirit in heart and mind, of human elements intruding into worship. I use the term *human* here in the sense of *carnal* or *fleshly*. It is possible that the truly Christ-oriented character that we should reflect can be stained by our seeking to glorify self instead of the Lord of grace.

• Discernment of the Spirit's presence and working in other people. This could take form in nonverbal communication between two believers who have not previously met, but who, on meeting, sense that the Holy Spirit is indwelling each other.

• Another manifestation of the gift might be differentiating between demon influence and mental illness. Many Christian psychologists believe both are possible, and God may use this gift to enable them to recognize the cause of abnormal behavior.

How can we tell if we have the gift of discernment? In addition to keeping in mind the general guidelines in chapter one, we can renew the functions of the ministry of discernment as recorded in the New Testament. Three categories emerge: *natural, spiritual,* and *gifted.*

Natural discernment is possible for every man, Christian or not. Sometimes we call it good judgment or horse sense—the ability to make wise decisions by observing and understanding. Some people have more of this than others, but it can be learned. All of us should be alert to do this.

Spiritual discernment comes to a believer as he grows in Christ (Eph. 4:14–15). It is connected to a great extent with knowledge of the Bible and with spiritual growth in our lives. It comes with a sensitivity to the Holy Spirit.

Gifted discernment is that which the Holy Spirit gives to some believers as a special gift, enabling them to serve the church as watchmen, to identify by supernatural insight what is not truth. Like many of the other gifts, this one can lead to pride and perverted use resulting in character assassination and harsh criticism. This will not happen if we remember that all gifts are of grace and for the benefit of the church and must be exercised in love.

10
Mercy and Hospitality

Part of the work of Mother Theresa and the nuns associated with her in India is to pick up the dying from the streets of Calcutta and bring them to a building where they can die knowing someone cares for them. Many die; but some survive and are cared for. "We want them to know," Mother Theresa says, "that there are people who really love them, who really want them, at least for the hours that they have to live; to know human and divine love. There is always a danger, if we forget for whom we are doing it. Our works are only an expression of our love for Christ. . . . To us what matters is an individual. . . . Every person is Christ for me."

W. A. Criswell links mercy, exhortation, and giving in a group which he calls the "sympathy of heart" gifts, the "precious ministering gifts of the Spirit."

One is the gift of mercy. Paul writes of it in these words, *ho eleonen hilarotati*, "he that showeth mercy, with cheerfulness." The Greek word *eleos* means "mercy, pity," especially in the presence of human misery such as is so often seen among the poor, the sad, the afflicted, the widows and the orphans. The New Testament Greek word for alms, *eleemosune,* is built upon the basic word *eleos* and is the origin of our English word "eleemosynary," an adjective used to describe charitable institutions and donations. The gift of mercy is the gift to sympathize with and to suffer alongside those who fall into grievous affliction (*The Holy Spirit in Today's World,* Zondervan, pp. 173–74).

The Gift of Mercy

I believe that we need to give greater emphasis to the less dramatic and spectacular gifts. Showing mercy or loving-kindness (Rom. 12:8) is a beautiful example of the personal care needed by thousands of hurting people in our congregations. When our theological debates about tongues and healings have left us cold and disunited, let us turn to the gifts of mercy and of hospitality in our efforts to minister to the church. This is the only real purpose of any spiritual gift.

Godet defines the gift well:

He that showeth mercy denotes the believer who feels called to devote himself to the visiting of the sick and afflicted. There is a gift of sympathy which particularly fits for this sort of work, and which is, as it were, the key to open the heart of the sufferer (*Commentary on St. Paul's Epistle to the Romans,* Zondervan, 2:293).

Showing mercy is a personal rather than official ministry. Some gifts are inseparably related to an office in the congregation—like pastoring or apostleship—but here we focus on a service dependent more on personal need than organization. Of course, it is possible that those who have this gift can be recognized by the church and designated to perform their service in conjunction with the total ministry of the congregation.

Some churches are responding to increased lay-leadership

awareness by assigning more pastoral duties to elders and deacons. The deacon-care program of the Southern Baptist Convention is one of the most detailed. It would seem that the gift of mercy is essential for men and women serving in *caring* ministries. One pastor describes his experience with a deacon-care program in these words:

In the church I am now serving, each deacon is assigned a proportionate number of families within the congregation. These families are under his care for a given year. In addition to interest and concern from the pastor and the church staff, each family has a deacon who will offer special friendship as the need arises ("Helping When There's a Cry for Help," *Church Administration,* Sept. 1973, p. 6).

Nothing in Scripture is inconsequential. We do well to note the exhortation Paul offers to those who possess the gift of showing mercy: "He who shows mercy, [let him exercise his gift] with cheerfulness" (Rom. 12:8, NASB). Matthew Henry writes:

A pleasing countenance in acts of mercy is a great relief and comfort to the miserable; when they see it is not done grudgingly and unwillingly, but with pleasant looks and gentle words, and all possible indications of readiness and alacrity (*Matthew Henry's Commentary on the Whole Bible,* Revell, 6:461).

The significance of the accompanying cheerfulness is seen by Cranfield to be

evidence of the special charisma that marks a person out for this particular service; but an inward *hilarotēs* in ministering will in any case come naturally to one who knows the secret that in those needy and suffering people whom he is called to tend the Lord is Himself present (cf. Matt. 25:31ff) (*A Commentary on the Holy Scriptures,* Oliver and Boyd, p. 33).

In the first century, as now, the gift should probably not be relegated to the relief of physical distress alone. Especially in today's chaotic society, we can see ample opportunities in which to minister this gift to those who are distressed in mind and spirit as well as body. The dimension of cheer is so important because this type of service (dealing with the sick and distraught) tends to reflect depression rather than joy. Hospital visitation is usually not the highlight of a Christian's week, but he dare not let it become mere duty, or worse, drudgery.

The word *hilarotēs* (cheerfulness) is the one from which we get our English words hilarious and hilarity. The context of this word here and in other places suggests the meaning of joy and cheer, certainly not humor and mirth at the plight of the sick and needy.

Remember that one test of a spiritual gift is the experience of joy in its use. The person who truly has the gift of showing mercy can tap the Holy Spirit's reserve of love and joy for his ministry to needy hearts. Grossmann suggests:

Many people shrink from the ill and weak; they consign these problems to an institution. In this area of daily life, mercy is a rare virtue. Wherever a person has this gift, he is a great hope for sick and neglected people. To be sure, merciful persons are quickly besieged by those in need. For this very reason it is important for all who have this talent [gift] to use it (*There are Other Gifts Than Tongues,* Tyndale, p. 27).

It is important to notice that no less than four of seven *charismata* mentioned in Romans 12:6–8 deal with practical ministry to needy people, an eloquent testimony to the service nature of the church and the service function of spiritual gifts.

The Gift of Hospitality

Hospitality does not appear in specific contexts in which the *charismata* are discussed, notably Romans 12:3–8; 1 Corinthians 12—14; Ephesians 4:1–16, and 1 Peter 4:10–11, but the word *philoxenia* meaning "love of strangers" does appear in Romans 12 and 1 Peter 4, and is separated from the crucial gifts context only by a few verses in Romans and by one verse in 1 Peter. The word is actually used five times in the New Testament (Rom. 12:13; 1 Tim. 3:2; Titus 1:8; Heb. 13:2; and 1 Peter 4:9). It is reflected in the ministry of Priscilla and Aquila, particularly to the Apostle Paul, but to other believers as well, since it is apparent that the couple's home served as the meeting place for the church.

Hocking offers four "insights about the gift":

- It is an evidence of an unhypocritical love (Rom. 12:9, 13).
- It is a qualification of a bishop (1 Tim. 3:2; Titus 1:8).
- It is easy to neglect this ministry and to miss many blessings (Heb. 13:2).
- The chief problem is doing it without complaining or grumbling (1 Peter 4:9) (*Spiritual Gifts,* Sounds of Grace Ministries).

"Offer hospitality to one another without grumbling" (1 Peter 4:9). The apostle has warned that the end is near, that Christians must be clear-minded and self-controlled in order to pray effectively, and that love must predominate in the corporate relationships of believers. "How does love cover over a multitude of sins?" The context speaks of believers having sufficient love for one another so that they will not notice each other's shortcomings. Also, the Christian who really loves will not speak publicly about his brother's sins. With that approach, the Holy Spirit commands through Peter, "*philoxenoi* one another without complaining." The noted commentator, Edward Selwyn, explains the passage.

The apostle is thinking rather of ordinary social life in the Christian communities, where [interaction] and meeting were essential to preserve the church's cohesion and distinctive witness, and where the Christians' households, in default of church buildings, were the local units of the church's worship (Rom. 16:5; 1 Cor. 16:19; Col. 4:15). This reference of the phrase to house-churches provides further an easy transition to the specific allusions to two of the main activities of the worshiping body—teaching and ministering (*The First Epistle of Peter,* MacMillan, p. 218).

All believers are to be hospitable; selfishness is not only tacky behavior; it is sin. We are to open our homes and welcome each other as guests for meals, overnight, or for whatever the need might be—and we are not to complain about the inconvenience it might cause. One of the interesting features of this gift is that implementing it today is little different than in the early church.

In Bible days, traveling was difficult. Inns were few, and those that were available were usually dirty and expensive. Often they were centers of immorality. This meant that when Christians journeyed to a new area, it was a great relief to have fellow believers invite them to stay in their homes. Today, though conditions have changed considerably, we should manifest the same spirit of hospitality. Christian courtesy never goes out of style (Richard DeHaan and Herbert Vander Lugt, *Good News for Bad Times,* Victor, p. 118).

I'm not so sure conditions have changed all that much. Traveling is still difficult. On holidays or during vacation seasons, hotels and motels may be filled. Many are dirty; most are expensive, and some are centers of immorality, however private it might be.

Flynn treats the English derivative in an interesting way. The main part of the word *hospitality* is hospital. Ancient travelers, whether pilgrims or businessmen, fared poorly when venturing beyond their own country. Thus, religious leaders established international guest houses in the fifth century. These havens were called "hospice" from *hospes,* Latin for "guests." With the coming of the Crusades, the importance of the hospice increased greatly. Pilgrims, crusaders, and other travelers found hospices, by this time run by religious orders, the only reputable guest houses of the era. Soon after the Crusades, most of these institutions began to specialize in the care of the poor, sick, aged, and crippled. During the 15th century, secular interests took over most entertaining of travelers, so the hospital restricted its function to care and treatment of the sick and handicapped. But originally it meant a haven for guests.

Though all believers are to be hospitable, some, perhaps more women than men, possess a special ability. The gift of hospitality is that supernatural ability to provide open house and warm welcome for those in need of food and lodging. Those who possess this gift should cultivate it (*19 Gifts of the Spirit,* Victor, pp. 109–110).

Think about your church. Whose home is always open to visiting missionaries, guest speakers, adult Sunday School class socials, parties for teenagers, and just about anything else that needs a home to make it work? Who is always ready to provide food when the believers get together to break bread in a social way? An even more crucial question—should it be you?

11
Miracles and Healing

Every other January, I spend a week with the spendid people at the Sudan Interior Mission Retirement Village in Sebring, Florida. My role is speaker at the Bible conference, but the benefit is largely mine as I enjoy companionship with these retired veteran missionaries. Collectively they represent hundreds of years of service to the Lord in various African countries. Each missionary tells how God worked His power—accounts of how He provided food when needed and safety in danger, and how the Gospel changed lives in the midst of pagan darkness.

It is quite common, even among believers in North America, to hear sincere reports of the healing hand of God in the lives of His people. A terminal cancer patient tells how a tumor suddenly went from malignant to benign; a tuberculosis victim details how, according to James 5, he called the elders of the church to pray over him and anoint him, and he became well; loving parents recall how a child seriously injured in an accident came out of a coma weeks after doctors had given up hope for recovery.

The question before us in this chapter is not whether the God of all grace and power *can* do miracles; no Christian doubts that. Nor is it whether those miracles can be in the realm of physical healing; no Christian should doubt that. The question is whether the gifts of working miracles and performing healings reside in people as instruments of God to carry out this aspect of His work.

The Gift of Miracles

"I believe in miracles," wrote John W. Peterson in a song with those words as its title, "for I believe in God" (Singspiration, Inc. 1956). At least 120 times in the New Testament we see the words *energēmata dunameon* (miracles) as the Father carries out His works of power through Jesus (Luke 4:36; Acts 2:22); through the power of the Holy Spirit in believers (Acts 1:8); and through the physical healings and other miracles performed by the apostles (Acts 3:12; 2 Cor. 12:12). The key passage regarding the gift of miracles is 1 Corinthians 12:10.

Not every healing is a miracle, nor is every miracle a healing (cf. the blinding of Elymas in Acts 13:8–12). And the word *dunamis* does not always refer to a supernatural *physical* manifestation of power. The Gospel, for example, is a spiritual power producing salvation (Rom. 1:16), but is no less an evidence of supernatural power.

We might remind ourselves that not all supernatural power comes from God. The Antichrist will possess "all kinds of counterfeit miracles, signs, and wonders" (2 Thes. 2:9), a most interesting parallel to Hebrews 2:4, which tells us that the apostles furthered the message of God while He established their witness "by signs, wonders, and various miracles."

It is part of the nature of God that miracles come from His supernatural person. Yohn reminds us:

Miracles have existed from the first day of Creation until now though God has not publicly used miracles in every generation. The first man gifted to perform miracles was Moses, and throughout the history of Israel God raised up other miracle-workers. But after Israel returned from captivity to Jerusalem, the revelation, the prophets, and the miracles "closed" for 400 years. When Jesus came to earth, new revelation, new prophets, and miracles became public information. Then, within a few centuries, another divine silence fell upon the world. Yet silence was broken after 1,000 years. And today, miracles are again occurring, though they may differ in kind and scope (*Discover Your Spiritual Gift and Use It,* Tyndale, p. 113).

Yohn writes about general miracles of God in the lives of His people, but he also refers to missionaries who have "testified that God has used them on occasion to cast out demons." Are we to view this as the gift of miracles reactivated in our day? Is it also possible that some miracles have been performed even in the so-called silent periods, but were not reported as they would be today with worldwide media coverage?

In keeping with our definition and purpose of spiritual gifts, only those "workings of power" which serve to edify the church are considered spiritual gifts. Obviously, evidences of Satan's power would be excluded, as would general prechurch miracles such as those performed by Moses, Elijah, or even Jesus Himself.

Nevertheless, it is impossible to draw sharp lines of demarcation between Christ and the apostles or between Christ and the church. We continue His work in the world as the extension of His body. The same resurrection power of which He partook is in some way available for our use.

In what way? Can we see evidence that the gift of working miracles is possible in the 20th century? Or must we conclude with some that this and other gifts ceased at the end of the first century?

Dogmatism and closed-mindedness should not characterize Christians serving a God who cannot be limited by the prohibitions of His own creation. The very definition of miracles denotes a supernatural intervention (in the case of a spiritual gift, an intervention of God) into the ordinary course of nature.

The emphasis is always on the Source of the power—the worker is an implement in the hands of God. Godet puts it well: "The persons on whom these gifts are bestowed, not having any importance in themselves, do not count, so to speak (*Commentary on St. Paul's First Epistle to the Corinthians,* T. and T. Clark, p. 2:226).

What were some of the miracles (other than healings) which were a part of the life of the early church? We find judgment on unfaithful Christians (Acts 5:5-11); exorcism of demons (8:6-7); resurrections from the dead (9:36-42); and deliverances from danger (28:1-6).

Do Christians today have power from the Holy Spirit to raise people from the dead? I do not know. Even if we scale down reports from missionaries and national leaders around the world, there are cases which defy natural explanation.

Is there evidence of genuine exorcism today? I do not know, but a missionary friend of mine, who is not given to fanciful exaggerations of his ministry, testifies that God has used him in this way. Another highly respected evangelical pastor reports similar experiences.

Is it ever possible that God gives a jungle missionary a unique and clearly supernatural power to shake off diseases and dangers which threaten his survival? I do not know. But Paul's experience with the poisonous snake on Malta may have parallels today.

Some will argue that to suggest the possibility of the gift of miracles being operative today opens the door to an endless parade of charlatans, to say nothing of those who exercise Satan's power. To be sure, that danger is real, but no more real than the opportunity for Marjoe to bilk unsuspecting thousands of their money through an unscrupulous peddling of a quasi gift of evangelism.

We cannot be guided in our understanding of spiritual gifts by a fear born of unhappy experiences nor an exegesis which results from hermeneutical myopia. Of course, such a rule must apply to the positive evidences of any gift as well. The only dependable criterion is the text of God's truth itself, and there is no portion of Scripture which offers a clear statement that the gift of miracles completely ceased in the church or, if it did, that God could not restore it in any age in which He chose to do so. Remember, that spiritual miracles are as much the working of power as their more visible physical counterparts.

The Gift of Healing
In attempting to honestly treat all the spiritual gifts listed in the Bible, one runs into difficulty with two or three, and the gift of healing is one of them. The difficulty arises primarily because of the various interpretations held within the evangelical camp. Viewpoints are often marked by extremes. Consider the following popular approaches to the gift of healing:

• Anyone with the gift of healing has the ability to heal at will.

• Healing is entirely dependent on the faith of the sick person.

• The gift of healing was only for New Testament times.

Part of the problem stems from the abuse and perversion of many self-styled "healers." Even though there are as many false teachers promoting cultic heresy, few people question the reality of the gift of teaching. Emotions run high for and against almost every interpretation of healing.

The word for "healing" is *iama,* which appears in 1 Corinthians 12:9, 28, 30. These are the only New Testament uses of the word, though it is common in the *Septuagint* (Greek version of the Old Testament). Kittel describes it well within its biblical context:

> The gift of healing is an operation of the name of the exalted Christ. To put the same thing in another way, it is an operation of the ascended Lord through the Spirit (Acts 9:34; Rom. 15:18). It does not belong to the essence of the Christian state. It is an individual gift of grace (*Theological Dictionary of the New Testament,* Eerdmans, 3:213–14).

From Kittle's definition and more important, from New Testament patterns, it is clear that only Christ has authority to heal, and only He can direct how that authority should be used. To properly understand this fact frees the church from demanding that everyone be healed, and from making lack of faith the reason for failure.

It is worth noting that the plural is used each time the expression appears: that is, *gifts of healing* (1 Cor. 12:9, 30). Hillis suggests the implication that "each separate healing is a separate gift" (*Tongues, Healing, and You,* Part 2, Baker, p. 9). Stedman, on the other hand, refers the plural to "healing at every level of human need: bodily, emotionally, and spiritually" (*Body Life,* Regal, p. 43). Perhaps this latter suggestion is closer to the thrust of the text, though reputable commentators support both views.

It is interesting that the specification *gifts* always appears with *healings* in the text of 1 Corinthians 12 (*charismata iamaton*). A related word *therapeuō,* serves as a base for our English words "therapy" and "therapeutic." It primarily denotes the care of the sick and is commonly used by Luke. Criswell links the words in interpretation, suggesting that there is no difference.

He also sees contemporary fulfillment in the proper handling of modern medical care.

The two different Greek verbs used and the plural pronouns used have tremendous significance. Modern movements of hostility to medicine are mistakes and unscriptural. To disregard means of healing is like a farmer who prays for a harvest, but who sits down to see God do it alone. God has given to us means of healing as well as the desire to be healed. Medicines come from Him. Without His creative work they would not be in existence in this earth. Penicillin has been here from the dawn of time. It is just now that we have discovered it (not invented it). God made it. If you are sick in eye, or tooth, or ear, or body, trust in the Lord and call for "the beloved physician," a Doctor Luke to prescribe and a Preacher Paul to pray. That is the way to get well (*The Holy Spirit in Today's World,* Zondervan, p. 205).

Available Today?

The crucial, practical question remains: Are the "gifts of healings" available today? Like Tevye, I can confidently proclaim, "I don't know," but again I have to say that blatant dogmatism either affirming or denying existence of any gifts is a tenuous position. On a trip to Southeast Asia some years ago, I talked with Indonesian students at the Singapore Bible College who claimed to have seen many incidents of physical healing during that country's revivals.

Others, among them theologians Walvoord and Ryrie, take the position that healing "ceased as a gift with the passing of the apostles" (*The Holy Spirit,* Dunham, p. 180).

Some writers choose a cautious middle ground, and I prefer to cast my lot with them. Stedman, for example, claims that physical healing "is a rare gift today, infrequently bestowed."

In responding to the question, Why? he suggests, "It is not the will of the Spirit for it to be given in these days as widely as it was in the early church" (*Body Life*, p. 44). Stedman does see ample evidence of the gift of healing at the mental and emotional levels of disease.

A similar view is expressed by international Bible teacher Alan Redpath:

Healing is a gift, and I believe without any shadow of doubt God has given it to some—the ability to command disease to be removed from a human body in the name of the Lord. But I believe that for every 10 who practice the gift, probably only 1 has it in the sovereignty of God. There is no gift so trafficked with and commercialized today as this one (*The Royal Route to Heaven*, Revell, p. 142).

Fear of the fraudulent is a rational one widely shared among Christians. Yet we must be careful not to condemn by unwarranted sweeping generalizations. It is neither good logic nor good theology to say, "I never met a person who has the gift of healing; therefore, the gift is not given today."

In July 1973, *Christianity Today* published an exclusive interview with Kathryn Kuhlman, whom the editors called "the best-known woman preacher in the world." Any objective reader would be forced to conclude that her responses to penetrating questions represented a pleasant contrast to some of the ego-oriented "healers" we have seen in our generation.

Even if the gift of healing is operative today, it is biblically clear that massive works of miracles will not of themselves produce faith. Faith is a gift of God. Jesus did say, "Even though you do not believe Me, believe the miracles, that you may learn and understand that the Father is in Me, and I in the Father" (John 10:38). But He also said, "Because you have seen Me, you have believed; blessed are those who have not seen and yet have believed" (John 20:29).

The miracles of Christ on earth, faith-producing as they were, are apparently different in the economy of God than miracles of any other day. Today we are to walk by faith rather than by sight. "Believing is seeing" in the spiritual realm, and I am not prepared to argue that it cannot at times happen in the physical realm as well.

12
The Gifts and the Body

It is time to wrap up some conclusions, to clarify concepts that still may be hazy, and to emphasize certain important points.

Perhaps this can be done best by presenting three sets of propositions to suggest: first, the congregational setting for an understanding of spiritual gifts; second, the problems surrounding spiritual gifts; and finally, generalizations regarding use of spiritual gifts in the life of the church. At the risk of sounding dogmatic and over generalizing, I will begin the propositions with the words *every, no,* and *all.*

Every believer is a member of the body of Christ, which is the church. We cannot separate our understanding of spiritual gifts from the content of 1 Corinthians 12. In Paul's closely drawn analogy of the human body, he suggests that the members of the spiritual body are given spiritual gifts to exercise for the good of the whole body—the church. We cannot have spiritual gifts unless we are members of the body. Neither can we be believers and not be a part of the body described in 1 Corinthians 12.

Every member of the church has a ministry. Ministry (serving) is what spiritual gifts are all about. The four primary passages make this plain (Rom. 12; 1 Cor. 12; Eph. 4; 1 Peter 4). The ministry of Christ's body is, in reality, the ministry of Christ.

Every member of the body needs every other member. "So we, numerous as we are, are one body in Christ, the Messiah, and individually we are parts one of another—mutually dependent on one another" (Rom. 12:5, AMP).

Every member has at least one spiritual gift. The Greek word *ekastō* appears in 1 Corinthians 12:7, 11 and is best translated "to each other." How different our churches would be if we would stop being awed by the multiple gifts of others or being critical of how persons use or do not use their spiritual gifts. Stedman issues the call with clarity:

Once you realize that God Himself has equipped you with a uniquely designed pattern of spiritual gifts and has placed you where He wants you in order to minister those gifts, you enter into a new dimension of exciting possibility. This awaits any true Christian who is willing to give time and thought to the discovery and understanding of his pattern of gifts. He must also submit himself to the authority of the Head of the body, who reserves the right to coordinate and direct its activities ("Equipped for Community," *His Magazine,* Mar. 1972, p. 3).

Regulating Gifts in the Body
No gift today is of new revelation in the New Testament sense. Though the primary emphasis of Revelation 22:17–18 is to the text of the Apocalypse, the principle of a completed canon remains and there is no biblical or experiential reason to conclude that God has given new revelation in our day (Deut. 4:2).

I believe that the list of New Testament gifts is exhaustive. This does not mean that each gift is defined so specifically that we are required to limit it to only its first-century use. For example, exercising the gift of helps in our day may include carrying out that ministry in ways that would have been impossible in the first century.

On the other hand, I take issue with Mains when he talks about the gifts listed in the New Testament as being "illustrations."

If an all-inclusive catalog of gifts had been intended, I believe these passages would contain identical listings, especially since they are written by the same author. Just as I believe the various aspects of the fruit of the Spirit as identified in Galatians 5 (love, joy, peace, etc.) are representative—that is, the writer does not intend to include every possible virtuous quality—so the scriptural gifts of the Holy Spirit are to be understood in a similar way. Therefore it seems obvious to me that there are gifts not included in the New Testament listings, such as music, writing, painting, or dramatics (*Full Circle,* Word, p. 60).

I believe that this approach may lead to taking liberty with the text of Scripture. It also seems to cloud the distinction between spiritual gifts and natural talents.

No gift is precluded from appearance today, should the Holy Spirit's sovereignty so design. This is debated. Some say one way to rid the church of the abuse of certain spiritual gifts is simply to say that they do not exist today, and whatever one has when he claims these gifts must be explained some other way. I rather agree with Snyder that "such a position arbitrarily limits the operation of the Holy Spirit and the applicability of the New Testament to our day. There is no more warrant, for instance, to apply chapters 12 and 14 of First Corinthians exclusively to the early church than there is to limit the 13th chapter. Gifts and love go together" ("Misunderstanding Spiritual Gifts," *Christianity Today,* Oct. 12, 1973, p. 15).

There is no scriptural demand that a gift today take the same form it did during the early church. Nor is it necessary that gifts be linked with offices as was common in the first century.

No gift is required of all believers or given to all. The significance of the sovereignty of the Holy Spirit in giving spiritual gifts is at stake here. If we can judge a Christian's spirituality by whether or not he has received a certain gift, we will soon have divided ourselves into the *haves* and *have nots,* which was precisely the problem of carnality in the Corinthian congregation.

Neither can we command a gift from God. After clearly indicating in a series of rhetorical questions that no gift is the norm of every Christian (1 Cor. 12:29–30), Paul goes on to suggest that we should make efforts to have the more useful gifts. I presume this would allow praying for certain gifts, but never with the attitude that God owes us those gifts because we have asked Him for them.

No gift marks believers as uniquely spiritual or special. Where a New Testament gift was closely associated with an office, there was a distinction (the gift of pastoral ministry is an example), and the contribution which a spiritual gift makes to edifying the body appears to be the basic criterion on which it is judged in quality. Who receives what gift to make what contribution to the body is the prerogative of the Holy Spirit alone, and the only proper response is to humbly recognize how God's grace operates in the whole process.

Relevance of Gifts for the Body

All gifts serve the body, its upbuilding, and its ministry. Not everyone must use his spiritual gift only within the local church. When Paul talks about "the body," he is talking about the universal church. Of course, we experience the universal church through local churches in space and time relationships. The gift of evangelism may operate in the world, but its ultimate benefit is to the universal church. The gift of teaching may be exercised, for example, through child evangelism or a campus Bible class under the sponsorship of the Navigators or IVCF, but the body of Christ benefits.

All gifts represent supernatural levels of more common ministries. For example, every Christian is responsible to witness, but there is a gift of evangelism. Every Christian is responsible for teaching to some extent, but there is a specific gift of teaching. Every Christian can speak a word of comfort to his neighbor, but there is a gift of exhortation. Every Christian should participate in proportionate giving of his income, but there is a gift of giving.

Spiritual gifts are supernatural because they are given from a supernatural source, and operate on supernatural power. This is the difference between serving Christ in the flesh (or trying to do so) and serving Him within the sphere of the Spirit's filling in our lives.

All gifts are to be exercised in humility, unity, and love. The unique location of 1 Corinthians 13 between the strong gift passages of chapter 12 and chapter 14 highlights the necessity of *agape* ("love") in the exercise of spiritual gifts. No spiritual gift is of any merit if it is not exercised in love. In addition to the dynamic of 1 Corinthians 13, we repeat Peter's words: "Most important of all, continue to show deep love for each other, for love makes up for many of your faults" (1 Peter 4:8, LB).

All gifts are geared to personal ministry. To make it even more clear, one might say all gifts have to do with the way we serve people. We teach *people*; we help *people*; we lead *people*. We in the church must recognize the mutuality of the body. A spiritual gift does not belong to its recipient; it is Christ's, and each of us is a steward of it.

Perhaps no better words can be spoken to conclude a study of the spiritual gifts than these.

God has given each of you some special abilities; be sure to use them to help each other, passing on to others God's many kinds of blessings. Are you called to preach? Then preach as though God Himself were speaking through you. Are you called to help others? Do it with all the strength and energy that God supplies, so that God will be glorified through Jesus Christ—to Him be glory and power forever and ever. Amen (1 Peter 4:10–11, LB).